Organization Design:
A Practical Methodology
and Toolkit

Ronald J. Recardo

HRD Press, Inc. • Amherst • Massachusetts

Published by: HRD Press, Inc.
           22 Amherst Road
           Amherst, MA 01002
           1-800-822-2801 (U.S. and Canada)
           413-253-3488
           413-253-3490 (fax)
           www.hrdpress.com

ISBN 978-1-59996-152-1

Cover design by Eileen Klockars
Editorial services by Sally Farnham
Production services by Anctil Virtual Office

Contents

Acknowledgments

This book summarizes the over 25 years of experience I have had as both a corporate executive and a management consultant in leading organization design initiatives.

On a professional level, I am greatly indebted to the many clients and colleagues I have worked with who have had enough confidence in my abilities to allow me to lead these types of complex initiatives. I would also like to thank the executives and consulting colleagues who reviewed the manuscript and provided valuable content feedback.

Most importantly, I would like to thank those closest to me. I would like to thank my wife, Diane, and son, Dylan, who provide me love, encouragement, and inspiration. I would also like to thank my mother, Marie Recardo, for all her love, support, and sacrifice that has made me what I am today.

Lastly, I would like to dedicate this book to my father, John Recardo, who recently passed away. He instilled in me a strong work ethic and a commitment to excellence. I miss him more and more each day . . .

John Joseph Recardo
April 13, 1927, to November 23, 2007

Section I:
A Primer for Executives on Organization Design

Organization Design Defined

Restructuring, rightsizing, and *business design* are but a few of the synonyms managers use to describe the redesign of an organization's reporting relationships. Like many other management terms, *organization design* does not have a common, well-accepted definition. To give you some context for the framework and supporting tools, *organization design* is defined as a structured and analytically driven systems approach to configure an organization to foster achievement of valued business, customer, and employee outcomes.

Effective organizational design is accomplished through the alignment of the technology, organization, and process architecture to closely support the business strategy.

When is organization design most appropriate?

One of the most common mistakes made by leaders is to undertake an organization design project without doing appropriate due diligence. The targeted results are not likely to be achieved when you are addressing symptoms of the perceived business problem rather than the root cause. Listed below are the most common situations in which organization design is most appropriately used.

1. **The business strategy has changed.** One of the best practices discussed in the next section is that form follows function, or more specifically, strategy drives structure. Whenever an organization is about to embark on a fundamentally different strategy or when internal factors (e.g., introducing a new product or entering a new market) or external factors (e.g., competitor actions, industry trends, introduction of disruptive technology) dramatically change, leaders should evaluate whether their businesses' current organization structure is appropriate.

2. **The organization is under-performing.** The design of an organization can have significant impact on the revenue, cost, and profitability of a business. Sometimes redesign is necessary because of performance problems created by the poor alignment of the structure. Indicators of poor alignment include lack of coordination between interdependent work units, excessive conflict, unclear roles/responsibilities, poor work flow, reduced responsiveness/flexibility, and poor resource allocation. The number of organization levels, type of structure, and which functionality is centralized versus decentralized can affect any of the following:

   - Economies of scale/cost
   - Having the right people in the right place
   - Level of accountability/role clarity
   - Ability to leverage technology

3. **The organization is experiencing strong growth.** Certain organization structures, such as a customer/market structure, a matrix structure, or a product structure, more readily lend themselves to alignment around growth drivers, while others work particularly well in environments where transaction volumes are significantly increasing.

4. **There has been a change in leadership.** New leaders frequently use organization design as an initiative to "shake up" or transform the organization. The redesign efforts allow executives to transplant staff whom they have effectively worked with in the past, to remove "blockers," and sometimes to facilitate cultural change by inserting leaders who will model desired behaviors.

Organization Design Best Practices

Listed below are organization design best practices that should be incorporated into most projects:

1. **Structure always follows strategy.** An organization's business strategy should be used as the primary driver of any design efforts. Any future state structure must closely align with the strategy and cascade from it.

2. **Use a formal data-driven approach.** The success of design projects is greatly enhanced when organizations use a flexible and scalable process for assessment, design, and implementation. The most successful processes are data driven, capturing information from a diverse array of stakeholders (customers, best practices, etc.). This data discovery process is then used to objectively identify and select design alternatives.

3. **Use formal design principles and metrics to objectively assess alternative design options.** Successful design projects use design principles (e.g., aggressively apply technology to support core processes) and quantitative metrics (e.g., future state design will reduce headcount by 300 FTE) to evaluate design alternatives and later, during implementation, to evaluate the impact the selected design has had on the organization.

4. **Benchmark other related structures and incorporate learning.** There are a number of consulting organizations, trade groups, and professional organizations that have collected benchmarking information on a myriad of organization structures. Benchmarking can be used to get a design team to think out of the box; capture and integrate learning and mistakes from other organizations; and think about new ways to integrate technology, work flow, and structure.

5. **Establish and exercise discipline in using a PMO process and tools.** Success is to a great extent dependent on an organization's ability to set up a process and supporting tools that are not overly rigorous, but address the myriad of project details. This includes the following:

   - Appropriate project structure (number of teams and team membership)
   - Governance (team chartering)
   - Issue resolution
   - Scope control
   - Risk management
   - Project monitoring/reporting
   - Communications
   - Inter-team coordination

6. **Recognize organization redesign as more than boxes and butts.** All organizations are made up of an architecture that has three distinct elements: **T**echnology, **O**rganization, and **P**rocess. Technology comprises the data employees need to make decisions, the information systems hardware (e.g., telephony, servers, PCs), the production/operations technology that is instrumental in delivering your core product/service, and the software applications that interface with process and hardware. The organization comprises the administrative policies or business rules that drive behavior, business systems (e.g., planning, budgeting), human resource practices (i.e., everything from recruiting and rewards to succession planning), capabilities, and workforce competencies. And lastly the process element comprises the business processes, physical infrastructure of the business (e.g., the site strategy—number and location of work locations), and physical layout of work areas (e.g., the arrangement of offices and conference rooms). When redesigning an organization, it is critical to fully understand the "ripple effects" that any changes to organization structure will have on each of the elements of architecture. Success is dependent on crafting a solution that proactively aligns all elements of architecture with the business strategy.

7. **Identify and celebrate short-term wins.** An enterprise-wide design is akin to a marathon road race. To keep the various stakeholders engaged, it is imperative to identify, celebrate, and reward early wins. This will enhance your ability to sustain the new structure and ensure it is institutionalized.

8. **Proactively identify and address change management issues.** Most design projects have considerable people/organizational implications. Examples range from culture change and stakeholder engagement to communications and modifications to the rewards systems. The earlier these implications are identified and proactively addressed, the higher the success rate of these projects.

The Role of Executives in Leading/Sponsoring a Redesign Project

There are seven key roles an executive should take on when sponsoring organization design projects:

- **Create a burning platform.** One of the first steps in any well-conceived change initiative is to increase the "pain" people are feeling so that stakeholders understand the price of maintaining the status quo is more than the price of a new future state. Executives must communicate clearly and effectively the business case (what is broken) and future vision. An effective sponsor must actively demonstrate their commitment publicly, exercise their formal position power when needed, and meet privately with key stakeholders to ensure continued commitment.

- **Make sure organization design is the right medicine.** A common oversight that is made is to embark on a redesign project without having completed an appropriate diagnostic to obtain consensus on the symptoms versus the root cause of your problems. Often redesign is undertaken as the solution, but regardless of how well it is implemented, it cannot have the desired impact because it won't fix the root cause of your problem.

- **Ensure there is cascading commitment.** Focus sufficient time on identifying, segmenting, and prioritizing all the internal/external stakeholders who are likely to be impacted by the new structure. Starting with the top of the existing organization and working down, make sure you have identified and engaged "champions," informal group/thought leaders, and managers at each level in the organization. Blockers need to be identified and aggressively addressed or they will adversely impact the project.

- **Be candid with stakeholders to manage expectations.** Credibility is a key success factor for being an effective sponsor. In part, credibility evolves from being direct, honest, and upfront. If you have a preliminary future state structure in mind, then communicate it rather than asking people to work through a data-driven process that may take a design team in another direction. Currency can also be built up by identifying any "sacred cows" upfront. Lastly, expectations can be managed more effectively when quantitative metrics are used to guide the design efforts.

- **Don't circumvent the organization design process.** If you opt to use an objective, data-driven organization design process, don't intervene to change the design recommendations without just cause. The organization design process is a discovery process that uses different data streams (e.g., voice of the customer, best practices) and decision filters (e.g., design principles, design metrics) to identify and evaluate different alternative designs. If you circumvent the recommendations without just cause, stakeholders can perceive the process as manipulative and undermine the implementation of the new structure.

- **Provide adequate resources to ensure success.** Your commitment will be evaluated to a large extent by how closely your words match your actions. If the project is truly important, then appropriate budget, facilities, and talent will be made available to ensure project success.

- **Proactively and decisively address the myriad of change management issues.** By far, the number one key success factor in organization design projects is to identify and decisively address the myriad of organizational/people issues. These include the following:
  — Talent retention and manpower redeployment: identify key talent, execute a strategy to maximize talent retention, and develop a plan for manpower reassignment
  — Performance monitoring: develop metrics and use them to track the progress of the new structure
  — Change inhibitors: understand and address the sources/causes of resistance
  — Communications: target messages to key stakeholders and use "sensing" mechanisms to assess the effectiveness of communications
  — New skill acquisition: identify and address key competency gaps
  — Stakeholder management: ensure cascading commitment
  — Culture alignment: identify what cultural changes need to evolve over time so that the new structure will be successful
  — Role clarity: clarify roles, responsibilities, decision rights, performance expectations, and handoffs between interrelated functions
  — Rewards and recognition: provide rewards for desired behaviors and outcomes
  — Consequences management: administer sanctions for nonperformance

Understanding Resistance to Change and Strategies for Overcoming Resistance

Why Do Stakeholders Resist Change?

Understanding why and how individuals resist change is integral to addressing one of the more common derailers of project success. Listed below are the common reasons why individuals resist change:

- **Fear of future competence/job security.** Organization redesign projects almost invariably entail new skill or knowledge requirements. If organizations do not provide timely and targeted education, employees will become apprehensive regarding their future job security or job competence.

- **Lack of adequate rewards/punishments.** Human behavior tends to be directed toward self-satisfaction. A common oversight is the failure to identify the type of behaviors and output measures that should be rewarded and compare them to those currently being rewarded. If management does not either reward the desired behaviors or output measures or punish noncompliance, then employees have little incentive for embracing the change.

- **Stakeholders' perception that the new design will negatively impact them.** People don't resist change for the sake of change. If your boss offered you a promotion that provided you with more money and greater visibility, chances are you wouldn't resist this. Humans tend to conduct a subconscious cost-benefit analysis when faced with an organizational change. If they view themselves as net-net worse off, they tend to resist change. If they view themselves better off, they tend to embrace it.

- **Unclear expectations.** Most organizations do a poor job of communicating to employees. Employees are sometimes forced to base the cost-benefit analysis (discussed above) on incomplete or incorrect information. Unfortunately, many times their conclusion is based on perception, rumors, and spurious data that facilitate a wrong conclusion. Effective communication occurs in three directions (top-down, bottom-up, and horizontally). Significant effort must be directed to keeping the workforce apprised of the big picture and how the change will affect them. Management must also develop procedures/vehicles to actively solicit employee input and to address their ongoing concerns. Those organizations that do an adequate job of communicating the *what*, the *why*, and the *how* regarding the change have a better track record at change management.

- **More work.** New structures commonly require modifications to work processes, enabling technology, competencies, and individual roles and responsibilities. This usually means more work or responsibility for employees, with typically the same or less opportunities for reward or career progression.

- **Altering of a long-standing habit.** Human beings tend to be creatures of habit. As the old adage states, "It is easier to worship the devil you know (and are comfortable with) than the devil you don't know." Organization design initiatives frequently alter long-established habits relating to such things as work rules, job design, and limits of decision-making authority. During this process, individuals struggle with various amounts of uncertainty as they break away from what they are familiar with and comfortable doing.

- **Unresolved past resentments.** Organizations that have struggled with implementing change in the past frequently need to address unresolved issues before embarking on a new change initiative. Failure to address these lingering issues will almost invariably affect the success of the new organization structure.

- **Modifications of existing social interactions.** All organizations are composed of formal and informal groups. Those people who we regularly eat lunch with and the cliques we belong to are examples of social interactions that occur within informal groups. If the new structure significantly modifies long-established social interactions, resistance is likely to occur. This is because the needs (i.e., recognition, affiliation, ego) the informal groups were satisfying are no longer being met.

- **Poorly introduced change implementation.** Care must be exercised to determine the appropriate scope of introduction (e.g., pilot), speed of introduction, and amount of employee involvement. A redesign initiative that is introduced without carefully considering these variables will not have cascading commitment throughout the organization.

- **Insufficient resources.** A sure fire way to foster employee resistance is to ask them to embrace a new design and then don't give them the necessary resources to complete the task at hand. One of the key variables employees will use to judge management commitment is the sufficiency of resources allocated.

How do people resist change?

Understanding *how* employees resist change is considerably more difficult than understanding *why* they resist change. That's because the *how* comes in both overt and covert forms (See Figure 1).

Figure 1: Common Ways Employees Resist Change

Overt ways	Covert ways
Sabotage	Reduction in output
Overt opposition	Withholding information
Agitating others	Asking for more data or studies

It is much easier to identify employees who utilize overt ways to resist change. Once identified, the appropriate strategy and tactics can be applied to ameliorate the problem.

Over 70 percent of the time, employees use covert means to resist change. This provides the greatest challenge to management. These individuals tend to verbally espouse support for the new structure but are inwardly hoping to stall the change until the next initiative du jour comes along.

Tactics for Reducing Resistance

There are 13 different tactics to effectively reduce employee resistance to change. Each is discussed below:

1. **Communicate a clear vision of the future state.** The senior management team is typically in the best position to develop this vision. A well-developed vision will communicate something is broken while creating a sense of urgency for employees to act.

2. **Engage senior management to lead the effort.** Successful large-scale organization change only occurs from the top down. Middle managers and staff people simply don't have the authority to make the widespread change that is needed to ensure success. Senior management must act as role models and demonstrate their commitment personally. They must also clearly communicate their expectations and hold people accountable for success.

3. **Link the old to the new.** It is not uncommon for individuals to go through a process of mourning the past. Allow them to express their grief and loss. Avoid bad-mouthing the past, which will only foster defensiveness in those who either designed or maintained the "old way" of doing things.

4. **Modify appropriate elements of architecture.** Depending on the scope and complexity of the redesign, one or more elements of architecture may need to be modified to support the change. For example, if an organization intends to transition to a product-based structure, selected jobs would likely need to be redesigned, new applications may need to be developed or purchased to support the new structure, core and support process might need to be reengineered, and the physical layout of offices might need to be modified to incorporate more teaming.

5. **Create and execute a communication strategy.** In the early stages of the project, a stakeholder analysis should be completed and the learnings channeled into a detailed communication strategy. This strategy should accomplish three objectives: to communicate the desired future state, to solicit employee input during the design process, and to identify/address employee concerns/open issues during implementation. There are two critical things to avoid: constantly surprising employees (this creates anxiety and fosters mistrust or a lack of confidence in management) and promising what you can't deliver. A well-developed strategy will ensure the following issues are clearly articulated to employees:

   - The business necessity behind the change
   - The vision
   - Timelines, approach, and deliverables
   - What will change/not change
   - Who will be affected
   - Benefits from an organizational and employee perspective

6. **Demonstrate a quick win.** We live in a world where managers are evaluated in terms of quarters and not years. Superstars are only as good as last quarter's performance. If you want to ensure commitment, it is essential to demonstrate some tangible results in a 60- to 90-day period. This initial success will also help you overcome the "not invented here syndrome."

7. **Develop procedures/practices to equitably address the "losers."** Most change projects create three distinct groups of people: the winners, the unaffected, and the losers. Individuals who as a result of a new structure obtain enhanced status, responsibility, financial gains, or visibility are clearly the winners. Another group of employees will be either indirectly affected or untouched. The concerns and open issues from the winners and losers should be integrated into the overall design/implementation plan. The individuals who are the biggest resistors of change are those who are the most negatively impacted. It is important to develop special procedures or policies (outplacement assistance, education, more targeted and sustained communications, job reassignment, etc.) to equitably address this group.

8. **Foster cascading commitment.** Effective change requires individuals to take on the roles of champion and missionary. Champions are those people who have the position power to mandate the change, while missionaries are those individuals who actively help you make the change happen. Whenever possible, use informal group/thought leaders as missionaries. Successful long-term change occurs only when there are a sufficient number of champions and missionaries at *each* level of the organization.

   It is also important to remember that individuals from affected groups should be actively involved in the planning, designing, and implementation of any redesign.

9. **Modify the performance measures and rewards.** The most impactful things to focus on are how the behaviors and targeted results will change pre- and post-redesign. Without significant modification of metrics, recognition, performance management, and rewards systems, you can inadvertently reward the wrong things and make it much more difficult to identify and address "blockers."

10. **Provide timely education.** The identification and delivery of education is an integral part of any well-conceived redesign project. It is critical to identify the key competency gaps and then quickly deliver appropriate knowledge transfer to ameliorate these gaps. Benchmarking can be used to quantitatively identify how the organization compares with its competitors across a wide range of parameters. This can be used effectively to create dissatisfaction with the present state and create a sense of urgency for the change.

    As the education is broadened throughout the organization, it should focus less on general awareness or strategic issues and more on new skill acquisition. A significant portion of this second tier of education should be targeted to individuals in focal roles—key positions within an organization that must support the redesign for it to be successful.

11. **Supply adequate resources.** Resources can take the form of budget, facilities, equipment, putting the best people on the project, access to key leaders, and support from external experts. Projects are commonly evaluated in terms of their strategic

impact and complexity. Most of the larger organization design projects are high on both of these criteria. The success potential of these types of projects is considerably lower if appropriate resources are not provided in a timely manner.

12. **Don't send mixed signals.** The average employee today is much more sophisticated than those of yesteryear. Management must "walk the talk" in all of its actions and directives because employees have become adept at recognizing disparity between what is said and what is done. The greater the disparity, the greater the distrust. If employees believe management has a hidden agenda or is not committed, they will perceive the redesign to be another one of those programs that will go away after a short period of time.

13. **Replace key individuals.** As a last resort, it is sometimes necessary to reassign personnel who either don't have the needed skills/personal attributes or who choose not to support the new design. The ultimate way management can communicate their conviction and support is to replace "blockers" who want to scuttle an initiative.

An Overview of Our Organization Design Framework

The organization design methodology is organized into three distinct phases (define, design, and implement), with each phase broken down into tasks and activities. Each phase includes a brief description, a listing of the common deliverables and tools that are used, and a breakdown of the tasks to execute the methodology. The methodology takes into account that organization designs need to be aligned with shifts in both environmental and strategic direction. The methodology is based on a systems approach and therefore takes into consideration how structural modifications will impact the technology, organization, and process architecture.

The methodology and tools have been designed to provide a range of robustness so that it can meet the needs of managers, HR partners, and internal/external change agents. The framework provides flexibility to address projects ranging in scope from a single location within a function to enterprise-wide across multiple locations.

The methodology is meant to be a guide to those who see the need for improving organization performance and believe that the structure of the organization is an impediment. It can be used in conjunction with other related methodologies such as Six Sigma or change management. Not every step will need to be followed in rigorous detail depending on the complexity and scale of the organization design. Also many of the tasks are described in a linear fashion. This is done for simplicity in describing the process. However, organization design is an iterative process. Therefore, some information or decisions made later in the process can and should be used to enrich and/or change earlier decisions. Finally, the tools may need to be modified and tailored to a unique situation. The user of this methodology should feel free to adapt this framework.

Figure 2 depicts the organization redesign framework that is augmented by approximately 25 diagnostic, design, and implementation tools (see Figure 3).

Figure 2: Organization Design Framework

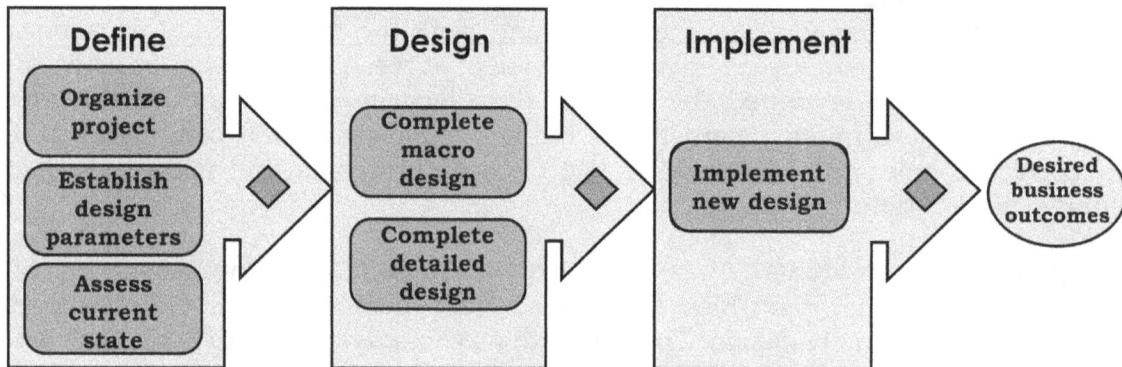

Phase 1: Define

Description:

During this phase, three major tasks are completed: organizing the project, establishing design principles and metrics, and completing an assessment of the current organization structure. Additionally, sufficient attention needs to be directed at fully understanding/confirming the business strategy, the demands the external environment is making on the organization, and the implications on the future state organization structure. Lastly, a detailed assessment of the organization structure is completed to understand the strengths/weaknesses of the current structure, identify functionality desired in the future structure, and understand the key gaps between the business strategy and the current organization structure.

Phase 2: Design

Description:

During this phase, the macro design and detailed design of the future state organization structure are completed. Key components of the macro-level design include benchmarking other similar structures, identifying alternative structures, selecting the high-level design, understanding the impacts of the high-level design, and identifying functionality to outsource. The key components of the detailed design include designing the operating units; identifying methods to facilitate interdependent units in working together; completing the design of jobs; and aligning the technology, organization, and process architecture.

Figure 3: Listing of Organization Design Tools

Tool	Define Phase			Design Phase		Implement Phase
	Organize Project	Establish Design Parameters	Assess Current State	Complete Macro Design	Complete Detailed Design	Implement New Design
Team competency matrix	●			●		●
Talent assessment and retention planning template	●			●	●	●
Human capital redeployment primer	●			●	●	●
Chartering template	●			●	●	●
Backwards imaging		●				
Design principles/metrics template		●				
As-is interview protocol			●			
Current structure review template			●			
Operating unit template			●		●	
Risk analysis tool			●	●	●	●
Overview of common organization structures				●	●	
Business case template				●	●	
Operating unit template				●		
Function/process relation-ship map			●			
Impact analysis template				●	●	
Employee selection guidelines				●	●	●
Design alternative decision matrix				●	●	
Role-to-job map				●	●	
Design/implementation challenge questions					●	
RCI chart	●				●	
Staffing estimation template					●	
Coordinating mechanisms template				●	●	
Service-level agreements				●	●	●
Standard operating procedures				●	●	●
Position profile					●	●

Phase 3: Implement

Description:

During the final phase, the new design is tested, leadership and key positions are filled, appropriate education is delivered, and the design is fully implemented. A number of key change management activities are also completed during this phase to ensure the success of the organization design.

Section II:
Organization Design
Methodology

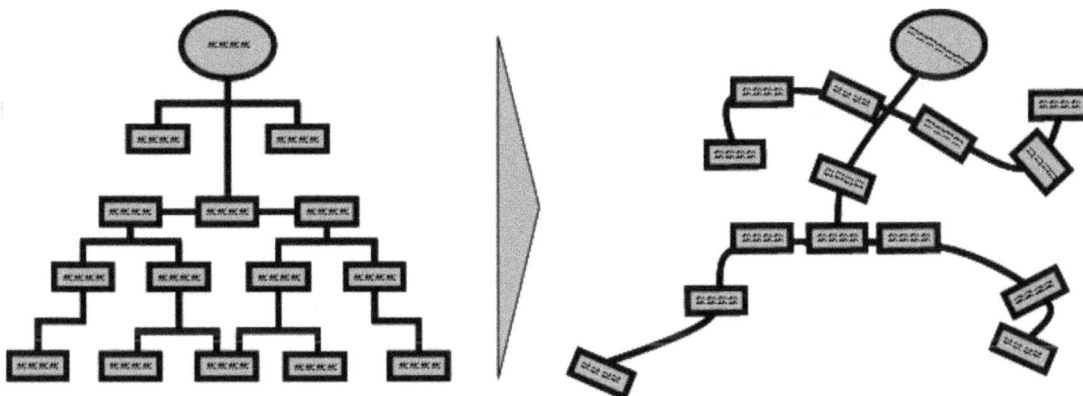

Methodology Overview

As discussed in Section I, the organization design methodology is organized into three distinct phases (define, design, and implement), with each phase broken down into tasks and activities. Each phase includes a brief description—a listing of the common deliverables and tools that are used. The methodology takes into account that organization designs need to be aligned with shifts in both market and strategic direction. The methodology is based on a systems approach and therefore takes into consideration how structural modifications will impact the technology, organization, and process architecture.

The framework provides flexibility to address projects ranging in scope from a single location within a function to enterprise-wide across multiple locations.

The methodology is meant to be a guide to those who see the need for improving organization performance and believe that the structure of the organization is an impediment. Not every step will need to be followed in rigorous detail depending on the complexity and scale of the organization design. Also many of the tasks are described in a linear fashion. This is done for simplicity in describing the process. However, organization design is a discovery and iterative process. Therefore, some information or decisions made later in the process can and should be used to enrich and/or change earlier decisions. Finally, the tools may need to be modified and tailored to a unique situation. The user of this methodology should feel free to adapt this framework.

The Toolkit

There are a number of tools in Section II. Most tools include a brief description, when the tool is most likely used in the organization design methodology, the steps for effectively using the tool, a completed example, and a blank template that can be used to support a real-world organization design project.

Phase 1: Define

Description:

During this phase, three major tasks are completed: organizing the project, establishing design parameters, and completing an assessment of the current organization structure.

An underlying assumption of the methodology is that the future state organization structure is driven by the business strategy. Therefore, sufficient attention needs to be directed at fully understanding the business strategy, the demands the external environment is making on the organization, and the implications on the future state organization structure. Lastly, a detailed assessment of the organization structure is completed to understand the strengths/weaknesses of the current structure, identify functionality desired in the future structure, and understand the key gaps between the business strategy and the current organization structure.

Common Deliverables	Common Tools
• Team charter(s)	• Chartering template
• Talent retention process and plan	• Talent assessment and retention planning template
• Human capital redeployment plan	• Human capital redeployment primer
• Stakeholder engagement plan	• Risk analysis tool
• Risk management plan	• Backwards imaging
• Communication plan	• Design principles/metrics template
• Vision statement	• As-is interview protocol
• Design principles/metrics	• Operating unit template
• Summary of current organization design	• Function/process relationship map
• Voice of the customer summary	

Organize Project

1.0 Establish project governance.

1.1 Establish PMO process, tools, and templates.

1.2 Clarify the role of the consultant (**doctor/patient:** provide the solution; **facilitator:** facilitate and provide guidance around the process).

1.3 Specify levels of structure (steering committee, organization design team(s), change team, etc.) required for overseeing, guiding, conducting, and implementing the organizational design.

1.4 Select members for each team (identify key individuals to engage in the process).

1.5 Complete team charter to clarify:
  - Performance expectations
  - Deliverables
  - Underlying constraints/assumptions
  - Scope (what's in/out of scope)
  - Roles/responsibilities/decision-making authority levels
  - Detailed project plan
  - Budget/resource requirements

1.6 Develop overall project milestone chart, noting critical path and interdependencies.

Common Tool:
  - Chartering template

Common Deliverable:
  - Team charter

2.0 Complete initial assessment of impacts that redesign will have on talent and human capital.

2.1 Develop definition of key talent.

2.2 Confirm goals of the organization design and identify the specific competencies that are critical to ensuring continued success of the business.

2.3 Force rank talent.

2.4 Categorize all employees into the following categories:
  - Strong performer, must retain
  - Okay in present job but needs development
  - Should be in job with less scope
  - Displace immediately

2.5 Complete talent loss forecast.

2.6 Identify retention strategies and develop a customized retention plan for each key talent.

2.7 Review current severance/displacement policies.

2.8 Develop a process/policy for how you will handle displacements.

2.9 Identify specific manpower redeployment options.

2.10 Review and refine plan as organization design advances.

Common Tools:
- Talent assessment and retention planning template
- Human capital redeployment primer

Common Deliverables:
- Talent retention process/plan for key talent
- Human capital redeployment plan

3.0 Identify impacted stakeholders and develop strategy for maximizing engagement.

3.1 Identify key stakeholders.

3.2 Assess each key stakeholder relative to the degree to which they are impacted by the organization design and their ability to influence the outcome.

3.3 Identify the key concerns of each stakeholder.

3.4 Develop the stakeholder engagement plan for obtaining a critical mass of commitment.

Common Deliverable:
- Stakeholder engagement plan

4.0 Identify risks and develop plan for mitigation.

4.1 Collect and analyze data relative to project risks.

4.2 Organize the risks into themes or categories (technology, process, organization, etc.).

4.3 Prioritize the risks according to the probability of occurrence and impact on the success of the redesign.

4.4 For the most critical risks, develop an action plan that either eliminates, delays, or reduces the probability/impact of key risks.

4.5 Make sure that you have linkages in place between the stakeholder assessment, communications plan, PMO, and risk management plan so that all are aligned.

4.6 Periodically update the risk management plan to incorporate project learnings.

Common Tool:
- Risk analysis tool

Common Deliverable:
- Risk management plan

5.0 Design/execute targeted communications.

5.1 Integrate learnings from stakeholder analysis and risk management into the design of the communication plan.

5.2 Develop a communication plan that addresses the following:
- Key messages for each stakeholder group
- Channels (town halls, newsletters, videotapes, etc.)

- Dates
- Responsibilities
- Feedback mechanisms (How will the learnings be integrated back into the risk management plan, commitment plan, PMO, etc.?)
- Communications effectiveness (Were communications interpreted correctly, timely? Information of interest/use and believable?)

5.3 Identify a strategy to counteract rumors.

Common Deliverable:

- Communication plan

6.0 Complete management review.

6.1 At the end of this task, ensure that there is a clear understanding of the following:

- The business imperative that is driving the need for an organization design
- A governance process for overseeing, guiding, supporting, and approving the organization design
- A project management plan with definition of the specific approach and needed resources
- An understanding of the key talent and a plan for retaining them
- A plan on how to address human capital re-assignment
- A risk management plan
- A communication plan

6.2 Have management reviews occur for each key deliverable.

Establish Design Parameters

1.0 Review strategic direction.

1.1 Review the following:

- Vision/mission
- Key challenges organization is facing
- Strategic plan/strategic imperatives/strategy map
- Business model
- Business drivers
- Metrics (note trends of key metrics and those that may have structural implications)

2.0 Review environmental demands.

2.1 Review the following:

- Industry trends/competitor moves
- Customer/market demands
- Opportunities
- Threats

2.2 Fully understand implications of opportunities/threats on structure.

3.0 Develop vision of future organization design (situational).

 3.1 Develop vision statement of future state organization design.

 3.2 Review vision statement with key stakeholders.

 3.3 Finalize vision.

 3.4 Use vision of the future organization design as an input into the crafting of the design principles and metrics.

 Common Tool:
 - Backwards imaging

 Common Deliverable:
 - Vision statement

4.0 Develop design principles and metrics.

 4.1 Brainstorm a list of potential design principles.

 4.2 Prioritize the list into "nice to haves" and "must haves."

 4.3 Develop a final list of design principles not to exceed eight principles.

 4.4 Translate design principles into five or less qualitative and quantitative metrics.

 4.5 Confirm appropriateness of design principles after you have collected voice of customer data, best practices, and strengths/weaknesses of current structure.

 Common Tool:
 - Design principles/metrics template

 Common Deliverables:
 - Design principles
 - Design metrics

5.0 Complete management review.

 5.1 At the end of this task, ensure that there is a clear understanding of the following:
 - Where the business is heading and the challenges it is facing
 - A vision of the future organization design
 - Design principles/metrics

Assess Current State

1.0 Review current organization structure.

 1.1 Review type of structure.

 1.2 Review number of organizational levels.

 1.3 Review spans of control.

 1.4 Understand flow of work across current structure.

 1.5 Collect/analyze structural cost data.

 1.6 Review strengths/problems.

Common Tools:
- As-is interview protocol
- Operating unit template
- Function/process relationship map

Common Deliverable:
- Summary of current organization design with strengths/weaknesses and opportunities for improvement

2.0   Review current process architecture.

2.1   Understand in detail information and process flows.

2.2   Identify process performance gaps where process is not closely aligned with the structure and strategy.

2.3   Identify shortfalls.

2.4   Catalog current infrastructure (number of facilities, location, size, site strategy, etc.).

3.0   Review current technology architecture.

3.1   Review current database configuration.

3.2   Review existing applications.

3.3   Review technology/hardware capabilities.

3.4   Identify IM shortfalls/limitations.

4.0   Collect voice of the customer data.

4.1   Solicit input from internal and external customers about their perceptions of the current organization design.

4.2   Identify their
- likes/dislikes;
- value of products/services;
- desired functionality;
- improvement suggestions.

4.3   Use voice of customer data to confirm/amend design principles and metrics.

Common Deliverable:
- Voice of the customer summary

5.0   Update and execute project, stakeholder engagement, risk management, talent retention, communications, and human capital redeployment plans.

5.1   Review learnings from current state assessment and gap identification.

5.2   Update plans as needed.

6.0   Complete management review.

6.1   At the end of this task, ensure that there is a clear understanding of the following:
- Top strengths and weaknesses of the current organization
- A clear understanding of the gaps that the new organization design needs to address, including issues around structure, culture, processes, and technologies

Phase 2: Design

Description:

During this phase, two key tasks are executed: complete macro design and complete detailed design of the future state organization structure. Key components of the macro-level design include benchmarking other similar structures, identifying alternative structures, selecting a macro-level structure, identifying functionality to outsource, and developing a business case to support your design decision. The key components of the detailed design include identifying methods of coordination and aligning the technology, organization, and process architecture.

Common Deliverables	Common Tools
• Benchmarking summary	• Business case template
• Outsourcing summary	• Overview of common organization structures
• Macro-level future state organizational chart(s)	• Design alternative decision matrix
• Impact analysis summary	• Risk analysis tool
• Detailed organization charts	• Impact analysis template
• Job descriptions	• Staffing estimation template
• Defined coordinating mechanisms	• Operating unit template
• Updated process maps and information flows	• RCI chart
• Future state technology migration plan	• Employee selection guidelines
	• Role-to-job map
	• Coordinating mechanisms template

Complete Macro Design

1.0 Complete internal/external benchmark of related organization structure designs.

    1.1   Confirm the specific attributes you want to benchmark.

    1.2   Identify possible benchmark targets (internally and externally).

    1.3   Develop data collection templates.

    1.4   Collect data.

    1.5   Analyze data to identify learnings.

    Common Deliverable:

    • Benchmarking summary

2.0 Identify functionality to outsource (if necessary).

    2.1   Plan and facilitate outsourcing workshop; obtain consensus on nonstrategic functionality.

    2.2   Identify potential vendors.

    2.3   Complete financial analysis to confirm outsourcing decision.

    Common Tool:

    • Business case template

    Common Deliverable:

    • Outsourcing summary

3.0 Identify and evaluate alternative designs.

    3.1   Using the vision, design principles, and design metrics and learnings from benchmark analysis, identify several macro-level design alternatives.

    3.2   Evaluate three to five *primary* design alternatives using any or all of the following criteria:

        • Fit with future state design vision
        • Alignment to design principles
        • Alignment to design metrics
        • Degree to which design decreases/eliminates weaknesses in the current structure
        • Degree to which design alternative doesn't adversely affect strengths in the current structure

    3.3   Integrate the business case data from the next task to rank design alternatives.

    3.4   Select preferred design alternative.

    Common Tools:

    • Overview of common organization structures
    • Design alternative decision matrix

    Common Deliverable:

    • Macro-level future state structure charts

4.0 Develop business case.

4.1 Work with your finance partner to identify the most appropriate method for completing the financial analysis:

- Internal rate of return
- Net present value (NPV)
- Cost-benefit analysis (CBA)
- Discounted cash flow (DCF)
- Return on investment (ROI)

4.2 Obtain agreement on algorithm to calculate the chosen method.

4.3 Develop a risk assessment for each of the "finalist" design alternatives.

Common Tools:

- Business case template
- Risk analysis tool

Common Deliverable:

- Business case

5.0 Decide on high-level design.

5.1 Determine the type of structure.

5.2 Determine the number of levels and spans of control.

5.3 Begin macro-level discussion of coordinating mechanisms.

Common Deliverable:

- Macro-level future state structure charts

6.0 Identify impacts on technology, organization, and process architecture.

6.1 Identify impacts of structural changes on organization architecture:

- Stakeholders
- Management systems
- Culture
- Administrative policies/business rules
- HR practices
- Competencies

6.2 Identify impacts of structural changes on process architecture:

- Core processes
- Support processes
- Value chain

6.3 Identify impacts of structural changes on technology architecture:

- Applications
- Data access/format/availability
- IT technology/hardware
- New product technology
- Production technology

6.4 Identify the impact on the current physical assets:
- Asset locations
- Number of locations
- Configuration of locations
- Rationalize physical assets

Common Tool:
- Impact analysis template

Common Deliverable:
- Impact analysis summary

7.0 Design operating units.

7.1 Identify preliminary missions/purpose of each function and department.

7.2 Identify preliminary inputs, suppliers, outputs, and customers.

7.3 Define macro-level description of how core/support processes will be executed in the new structure.

7.4 Update process/function metrics.

8.0 Update and execute project, risk management, manpower redeployment, stakeholders, and communications plans.

8.1 Review project, risk management, communication plan, and business case.

8.2 Incorporate learnings.

8.3 Update plans.

9.0 Complete management review.

9.1 At the end of this task, ensure that there is a clear understanding of the following:
- A macro-level design of the new organization
- A project plan to develop the details needed for detailed design

Complete Detailed Design

1.0 Complete design of operating units.

1.1 Refine and validate missions/purpose of each function.

1.2 Refine and validate inputs, suppliers, outputs, and customers.

1.3 Develop detailed descriptions of how core/support processes will be executed in the new structure.

1.4 Update process/function metrics.

1.5 Develop detailed descriptions of coordinating mechanisms.

1.6 Create plan for migrating to future state technology.

Common Tools:

- Staffing estimation template
- Operating unit template

Common Deliverable:

- Detailed organization charts

2.0 Complete job design.

2.1 Group tasks into roles.

2.2 Cluster roles into jobs.

2.3 Identify competencies.

2.4 Update job descriptions.

2.5 Define staffing requirements.

Common Tools:

- RCI chart
- Employee selection guidelines
- Staffing estimation template
- Role-to-job mapping tool
- Service-level agreements

Common Deliverable:

- Job descriptions

3.0 Finalize methods of coordination.

3.1 Identify the type of interdependence between work units:

- **Reciprocal:** Certain outputs of each group become an input for the other group. Collaboration needs to occur in both directions (e.g., R & D and Market Research).
- **Sequential:** Outputs of one group become input of the other group (e.g., Manufacturing and Shipping departments).
- **Pooled:** Groups are relatively independent of each other, but contribute to the overall goals of the organization (e.g., holding company).

3.2 Determine appropriate coordination methods:

- **Rules, programs, procedures:** Develop SOPs, policies, and practices that specify the desired behaviors, govern decision making, and/or limit discretion in advance.
- **Formal hierarchy:** Appoint a common manager to oversee two different units.
- **Targets/Goals:** Specify outputs, goals, or targets to coordinate interdependent groups.
- **Networks:** Formal or informal vehicles for encouraging knowledge sharing across functions, businesses, and geographies. There are six common ways to foster networks: co-location; communities of practice (groups of employees that share common organizational interests); annual meetings/retreats;

training programs; rotational assignments; and technology/e-coordination (e.g., chat groups, e-mail distribution lists on intranet, Lotus Notes, Microsoft Exchange, instant messaging, group calendar management, shared databases).

- **Liaison roles:** An individual who serves as a source of information and expertise to advise a work group; rarely has formal authority; position is usually part-time.
- **Teams:** There are a number of different team configurations across a conceptual continuum from issue teams, cross-functional teams, and task forces to self-directed work groups. Teams can be either permanent or ad hoc, but their value is in pooling expertise, breaking down functional silos, and coordinating efforts of interdependent units.
- **Lateral processes:** These are the three to five processes that are mission critical and cut across multiple functions within the organization. These processes should be mapped and include metrics at the end of the process, where the process crosses functions, and where performance problems have occurred historically.
- **Integrator roles:** There are two common types of integrator roles: *managerial* (an individual who is responsible for taking a general management point of view in helping multiple work groups accomplish a joint task such as a project, brand, program, or account manager); *coordinator;* or *boundary-spanning* positions (i.e., chief learning officer) that ensure that the work of each unit fits and is aligned with the business strategy.

Common Tool:

- Coordinating mechanisms template

4.0 Develop plan to align culture to support new organization structure.

4.1 Identify desired values and behaviors.

4.2 Align Human Resources practices to evolve culture:
- Performance metrics
- Employee development
- Compensation
- New skill acquisition

5.0 Define changes to process architecture to support new organization structure.

5.1 Modify support processes to ensure that they support the new structure.

5.2 Modify core processes to ensure that they support the new structure.

5.3 Map information flows.

Deliverable:

- Updated process maps and information flows

6.0 Define changes to technology architecture to support new organization structure.

    6.1   Align hardware to support the new structure.

    6.2   Align applications to support the new structure.

    6.3   Align databases to support the new structure.

    Deliverable:

- Future state technology migration plan

7.0 Update and execute project, risk management, manpower redeployment, stakeholders, and communications plans.

    7.1   Update plans as needed.

    7.2   Identify any changes needed in these plans and update plan.

8.0 Complete management review.

    8.1.   At the end of this task, ensure that there is a clear understanding of the following:

- A detailed description of how each operating unit will function
- A detailed description of the changes needed for jobs, coordinating mechanisms, processes, and technologies to ensure that the new structure will function

Phase 3: Implement

Description:

During this phase, there is one key task that is completed: implement new design. A number of key change management activities are completed during this phase to ensure the success of the organization design.

Common Deliverable	Common Tools
• Training plan	

Implement New Design

1.0 Complete simulations or pilot test design to ensure desired functionality.

    1.1 Determine test method; testing can be done through simulation workshops or piloting new processes/design in one area of the organization.

    1.2 Test and readjust as necessary.

    1.3 Share key learnings from test method with PMO.

2.0 Create slates and evaluate candidates. (Depending on the level of involvement and speed of introduction, this task may be completed during the Design Phase, most likely during Complete Macro Design. In some instances, you might opt to select level 1 leaders who are then responsible for selecting their direct reports with the process replicating itself at each successive level.)

    2.1 Identify decision criteria for employee assessment (i.e., experience, competency, past performance).

    2.2 Develop a transparent and robust process for selection (multiple levels of review to remove bias, consistency of processes, qualitative vs. quantitative data, etc.).

    2.3 Identify assessment team/selection team; ensure understanding of the assessment process and tools.

    2.4 Generate employee assessment packets* for each employee being considered for a new role.

    2.5 Facilitate assessment discussions.

    2.6 Review assessment results against recent appraisal results; discrepancies should be discussed with the selected stakeholders.

    2.7 Submit assessments to selected stakeholders for review.

* An employee assessment packet includes an employee assessment form for each employee on a slate. This form should have the skills and leadership attributes from the role requirements populated to ensure standard assessment criteria.

Common Tool:

- Employee selection guidelines

Common Deliverable:

- Employee assessment packet

3.0 Select candidates.

    3.1 Execute employee selection process (it should incorporate objectivity, full participation, and open dialogue and be evidenced based and skill/behavior driven).

    3.2 Selection team reviews slate creation and selection guidelines, including:
- Role requirements and skills
- Number of positions
- Number of employees on slates

    3.3 Develop a plan to obtain the appropriate documentation from the meetings.

3.4   Develop agreements on how to handle contingencies, such as equal employee assessments.

3.5   Schedule selection discussions and manage logistics.

3.6   Facilitate selection discussions to ensure fair treatment of employees and legal compliance.

3.7   Complete employee slating form based on results from slating meeting.

3.8   Assist in development of communication plan to notify selected and non-selected employees.

NOTE: Once the selection decisions have been made, leadership approval is needed. This must be obtained prior to communicating any decisions to employees. Once approval has been obtained, the employees are ready to be communicated to and brought on board into their new roles. *Leadership approval must be obtained prior to any communication about selection decisions.*

4.0   Identify knowledge transfer to address competency gaps.

4.1   Develop/update training plan. Possible areas might include the following:
- Competency gaps by role/function
- How each gap will be addressed (classroom education, on-the-job training, job aids, coaching, etc.)
- Detailed outlines of knowledge transfer requirements
- Make vs. buy decision

4.2   Identify and secure trainers.

4.3   Develop schedule.

4.4   Execute knowledge transfer.

Common Deliverable:
- Comprehensive training plan

5.0   Implement new design.

5.1   Execute training plan.

5.2   Monitor and continue to execute communication plan.

5.3   Monitor and continue to execute engagement plan.

5.4   Monitor and continue to execute risk management plan.

6.0   Capture lessons learned.

6.1   Evaluate organization design process and capture lessons learned.

An Overview of the
Common Organization Structures

Product Organization

Definition: Organized by the product/service provided, each with its own functional structure

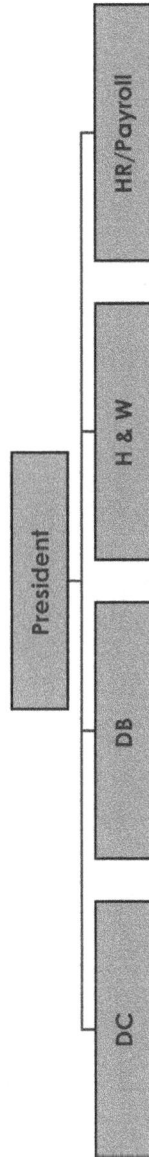

```
                    President
        ┌───────┬───────┬───────┬───────┐
        DC      DB     H & W   HR/Payroll
```

Advantages	Disadvantages	Most Appropriate When
• Decision-making authority and responsibility for results are focused under one individual • Resources required by the product line can be coordinated and controlled more easily • Expertise and knowledge in a particular product or market are developed • The organization can be easily extended as new product lines are acquired or developed • Shorter new product development cycle times • More responsive to environmental changes • Easier to focus people/resources and hold accountability • Improved knowledge about markets	• Does not appear integrated in the eyes of the customer • Company-wide policies and practices in each function are more difficult to control • Product development may be more difficult to coordinate when various product lines have to be compatible • Marketing is more difficult to coordinate when several products are being sold to the same customers or markets • Less depth or breadth within each function may result • Diminished focus on penetrating desired markets • Harder to coordinate efforts • Increased administrative expenses • Duplication of functional resources	• Products or services have relatively distinct technologies, processes, or markets • Product line volume will enable company to take advantage of any efficiencies of scale that exist • Products and/or their markets are rapidly evolving or changing • Product characteristics are more important in determining success than overhead cost control • Commonly used in organizations that operate in an uncertain and highly competitive environment, with short product development life cycles, wide product lines for separate customers, and low synergies across products

Functional Organization

Definition: Organized around major activity groups, R & D, HR, etc. (most common)

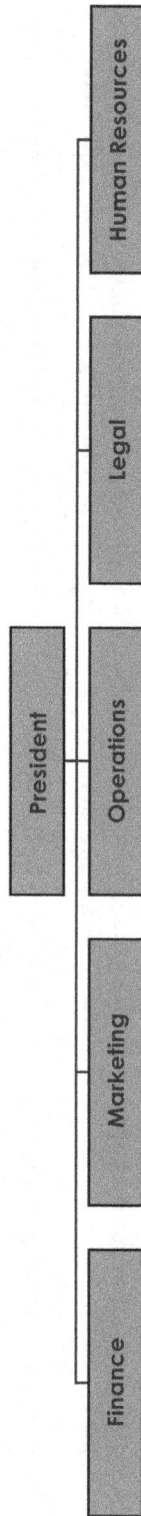

```
                    President
   ┌──────────┬──────────┼──────────┬──────────────┐
Finance   Marketing  Operations   Legal      Human Resources
```

Advantages	Disadvantages	Most Appropriate When
• Each function has clear responsibility and authority • All functional specialists are in one department —Easier control of function —Clear career paths/more specialization —Elimination of duplication of effort and redundancy —Better cost control within each function —Promotes in-depth functional expertise • Each major function is headed by a manager who reports to—and can advocate views to—top management • Fosters efficiency/economy of scale	• No one below the president has full P & L responsibility • Problem solving and coordination of actions that cut across several departments are difficult • Functional specialists often attach less importance to what's best for external customers and the whole business • General management perspective and experience are harder to develop • Lack of process focus • Silo orientation • Less overall understanding of the business	• Organizations are relatively small • Product line is relatively simple • Products, tasks, and markets are well defined and changing slowly • Overhead cost control and efficiency are keys to profitability (typically the case with commodity products in mature markets) • You want to maximize margins through leveraging economies of scale and functional expertise; works best with stable markets, narrow product lines, and well-understood customer requirements

Organization Design: A Practical Methodology and Toolkit

Geographic Organization

Definition: Organized around physical locations such as states, countries, or regions

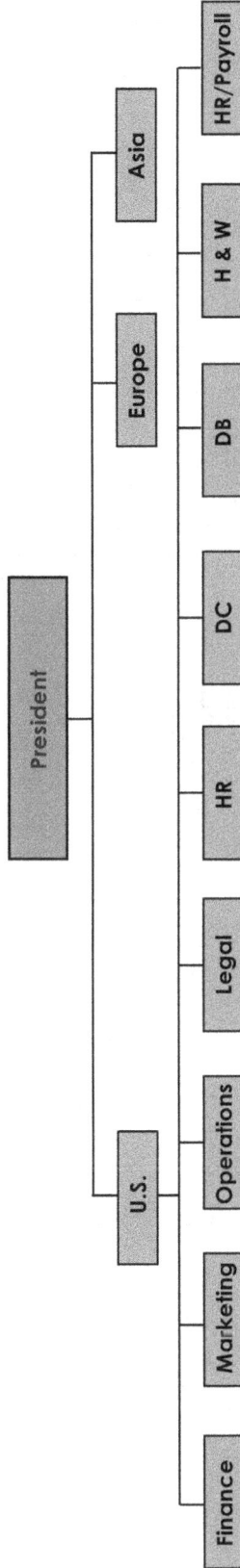

Organization chart:
- President
  - U.S.
    - Finance
    - Marketing
    - Operations
    - Legal
    - HR
    - DC
  - Europe
    - DB
  - Asia
    - H & W
    - HR/Payroll

Advantages	Disadvantages	Most Appropriate When
• One person has all the resources required to serve a region and is responsible for company performance • Regional differences in markets can be tailored to specific customers • Coordinating sales of multiple products or delivery of multiple services is easier • Regional units can serve as a training ground for higher-level general managers • Decision making is closer to customer and market knowledge and thus provides faster and better response	• Duplication of resources across regions may occur • Company-wide policies and practices in each region are more difficult to control • Another layer of management is required to run geographic units • Sales efforts or other actions that require cooperation across regions are hard to coordinate	• Products or services are produced and used in the same geographic area • Market has many customers who are primarily local • Regional market differences are important • Number of people required to deliver product or service is too large to manage effectively from a geographic distance • Organization wants to focus product/service delivery according to differences in geographic requirements, closeness to the customer is a KSF, and there is a low value to transport cost ratio

Market/Customer Organization

Definition: Organized around major market segments such as client groups, industries, or population groups

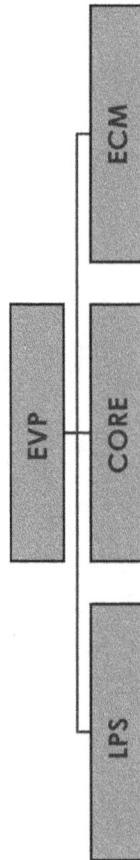

```
              EVP
    LPS       CORE       ECM
```

Advantages	Disadvantages	Most Appropriate When
• A depth of knowledge and expertise about a customer or market is developed • Product can be tailored specifically to particular customer needs • The delivery of diverse products or services to a given customer is easier to coordinate • Improved relationship management • Enhanced customer satisfaction	• Duplication of resources across customers or markets may occur • Setting priorities or allocating resources across customers may be difficult • Lost economies of scale	• Products or service requirements differ substantially by type of customer • Depth of knowledge and contacts by industry or customer are essential for success • Large volumes are being sold or provided to well-defined customers or markets • Diverse resources must be coordinated to meet customer needs • When you have well-defined customer segments with unique products/services, quick response and customer knowledge are competitive advantages

Organization Design: A Practical Methodology and Toolkit

Matrix Organization

Definition: Combination of functional and product/market structure (most difficult to implement)

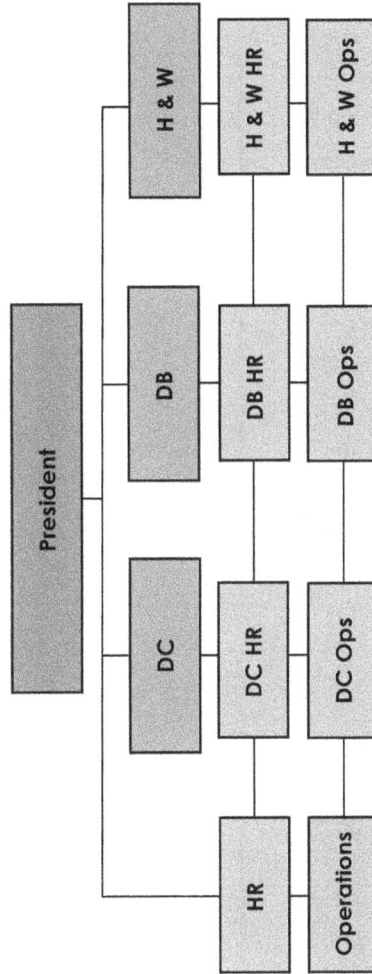

President

HR	DC	DB	H & W
Operations	DC HR	DB HR	H & W HR
	DC Ops	DB Ops	H & W Ops

Advantages	Disadvantages	Most Appropriate When
• Permits flexibility in putting together multidisciplinary task or project teams for as long or short a time as required • Both project management and technical specialization are provided • Overlapping team membership can be used to integrate several subtasks on an overall project	• Scheduling and management are very difficult • Excellent project management and interpersonal skills are required • There is no easy way to solve conflicting priorities • Uncertainties about responsibilities and career paths occur	• There are a large number of projects or tasks of varying length requiring multidisciplinary teams • There is a strong need to balance power at both technical expertise and programmatic integration • Appropriate when you want to focus on process innovation, reducing cycle times, cost, and working capital

Process Organization

Definition: Organized around core processes or technology such as supply chain, demand generation, etc. (very difficult to implement)

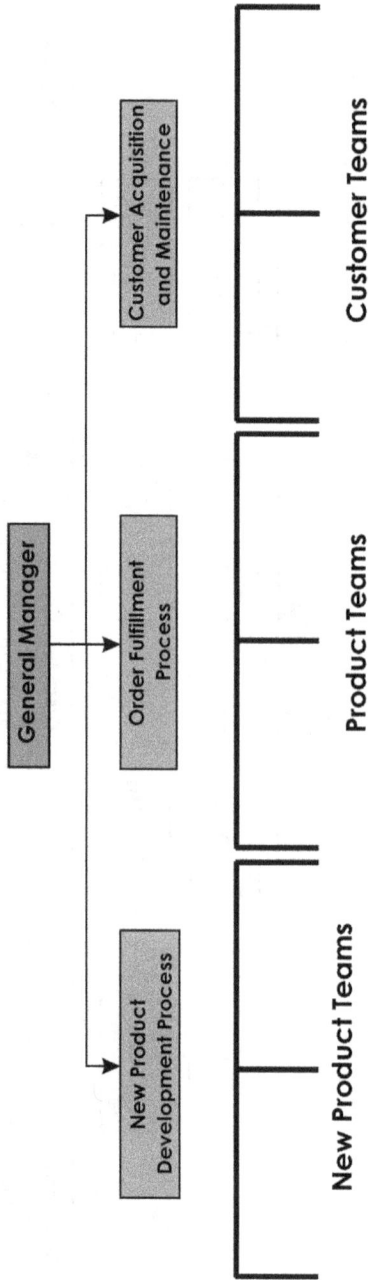

```
                        ┌─────────────────┐
                        │ General Manager │
                        └─────────────────┘
                                 │
        ┌────────────────────────┼────────────────────────┐
        │                        │                        │
┌───────────────┐      ┌──────────────────┐      ┌──────────────────────┐
│  New Product  │      │ Order Fulfillment│      │ Customer Acquisition │
│  Development  │      │     Process      │      │   and Maintenance    │
│    Process    │      └──────────────────┘      └──────────────────────┘
└───────────────┘
```

New Product Teams   Product Teams   Customer Teams

Advantages	Disadvantages	Most Appropriate When
• Improved accountability for a process from cradle to grave • Reduces functional hand-offs by defining work in terms of customer-driven processes • Improves coordination of similar efforts • Institutionalizes customer-driven process focus at highest levels of the organization	• People requirements are typically higher: greater breadth, tolerance for ambiguity, etc. • Results in the greatest amount of change—"turning the organization on its side" • Existing culture is a constraining variable	• Strategic focus is on process issues (e.g., flawless implementation) • Clients and employees are inclined toward process thinking • You want to focus on process innovation, reducing cycle times, cost, and working capital

Hybrid Organization

Definition: Combination of any of the other design options

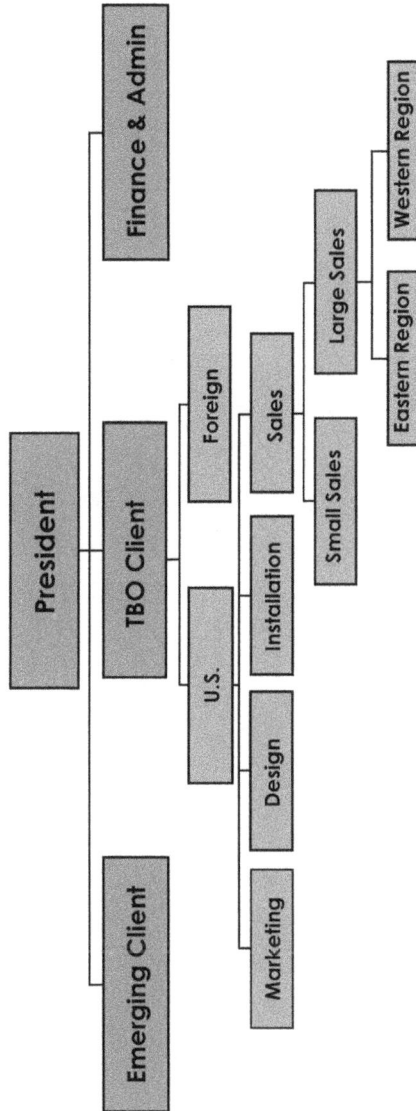

Advantages	Disadvantages	Most Appropriate When
• The form of organization is chosen based on the following: —What information is required —Who has the information —What resources and facilities are required —Economies of scale —Speed and flexibility of response —Need for integration of activities —Ease of management —Career paths and development of people	• Clear lines of responsibility and authority are harder to create in a hybrid than in a functional organization • It may be harder for both employees and customers to understand • Clear career paths to the top may not be provided • Increased conflict • Increased overhead	• No single form of organization meets the requirements of different parts of the enterprise

As-Is Interview Protocol

What it is and when should it be used?

The as-is interview protocol is designed to gather data on the current organizational structure. The interview protocol can collect a variety of information such as staffing levels, budgets, products and services offered, and interdependencies across different units.

This tool should be used during the Define phase when completing the Assess Current State.

How to do it:

1. Identify what decisions you plan to make as a result of the data-collection process.

2. Identify the stakeholders you would like to interview. By customizing and targeting the questions, you can also include suppliers and customers as potential data-collection targets to augment information collection from managers.

3. Provide some structure and guidance around how the data will be collected and analyzed.

4. Analyze the data for themes and drivers.

(continued)

Blank Template

Interviewer: _____

Date: _____

Interviewee: _____ Organization:_____

1. What functions/departments are included within the organization you manage? For each function/department how does it support the strategy of the overall business?

2. Can you provide me with a copy of the current organization structure chart of your organization? Can you walk me through the budgets for each of the functions and departments you are responsible for? How many full-time equivalents, contractors, and part-time staff do you have in each function/department you manage?

3. What metrics do you use to measure your overall organization and each function/department within the organization? Which measures are most important? What are the recent performance trends regarding each of the important measures?

4. What products/services do suppliers provide to each function/department you manage? Which ones are most important? What is your level of satisfaction regarding each product/service you receive (data, info, material, etc.)? What new services/products would you like from your existing suppliers that you are not currently receiving? Do you use any significant outside suppliers?

Suppliers	Importance (High, Medium, Low)	Satisfaction (High, Medium, Low)	Key Inputs

(continued)

Blank Template *(concluded)*

5. What key products/services does your function/department deliver to its customers? What percentage of resources do you allocate to delivering each product/service? Who are your customers? Which ones are most important? What products does each customer receive?

Key Product/Service	Customers	Importance	Headcount	% of Time

6. Specifically what changes would you make to the existing structure within each function/department? Overall? Are there any alternative service providers (can they be outsourced) for any of the key activities who can do it faster, more economically, or better?

7. What problems do you have with interfaces between your function and other related functions?

Backwards Imaging

What is it and when should it be used?

For large and complex organization design efforts, it is sometimes necessary to develop a vision that describes what the future state structure will look like. This should not be confused with developing a vision for the organization. This tool guides the team's thinking to focus on what people will be *doing* in the future state, rather than staying with a vision that is so lofty that few truly understand what the future will really be like when the organizational design effort comes to fruition.

Backwards imaging is an excellent way to help teams wrestle with the specifics of what the future state will be like in terms that can uncover both support and resistance. It asks people to describe the future as they expect to see it when the organizational design effort is successful and to do so in specific, behavioral terms.

This tool should be used during the Define phase when completing Establish Design Parameters. Visioning is situational depending on the scope (location vs. enterprise-wide) and it is an input into design principles and metrics.

How to do it:

1. Team members are asked to individually imagine a time in the future when the organizational design is completed. Often this is framed as the end-of-the-year party when the team is celebrating its success. Or ask individuals to think forward to a front-page *Wall Street Journal* article that describes the success of the organization redesign project. If the business completed an organizational redesign flawlessly, what would the article say? When people have had the opportunity to create their own article, they can discuss their thoughts as a group and begin to build the future state organization design vision.

2. With this "picture" of the future in mind, team members then try to describe what they see, hear, or feel as they observe key stakeholders and other constituents behaving in the changed state.

3. Compile the various views of this future state from individual team members and discuss and debate similarities and differences. Use learnings from the stakeholder assessment you created earlier to test this view of the future on key stakeholders and the organizational design effort sponsor.

4. OPTION: Some teams may wish to actively solicit ideas from key stakeholders as a way of building this picture, rather than doing the work themselves and then sending the vision out for comment and critique.

5. Make sure that the vision meets four key criteria:
   - The vision is clear.
   - The vision is easy to communicate.
   - The vision is compelling.
   - The vision is measurable.

(continued)

Completed Example

> We are a team-based organization that is organized around core processes that are tightly aligned to our key customer segments. Our employees exhibit initiative, take calculated risks, have a sense of urgency, and are strongly focused on impacting the bottom-line results of the organization.

Business Case Template

What is it and when should it be used?

A business case is used to quantitatively prioritize design alternatives. Used in conjunction with the design principles and design metrics, a business case can be used to calculate the benefits and costs of the "short list" design alternatives. A business case is best used in conjunction with other decision variables, but **not** as the primary criteria to select one design alternative over another one.

Business cases are most commonly used during the Design phase during the Macro and Detailed Design activities. The business case should show where the organization is today and compare it to where the organization is expected to go in the future. It is used to gain the support and commitment from key stakeholders.

How to do it:

1. To build the business case, refer to the guidelines listed below and work closely with your finance partner to build and analyze the business case. After building the business case, have a management review session for an initial review of the proposed organizational design.

I. Guidelines
What are the major ***categories*** of costs and benefits (e.g., infrastructure, outside vendors)?
For each category of benefits and costs, brainstorm potential line items. Potential costs associated with infrastructure can be such things as moving expenses, the purchase of new real estate, site assessment, or rent during the transition.
Finalize the appropriate cost and benefits categories and line items you will use to create the business case.
Populate the business case with data. Check for reasonableness. When documenting benefits, also take note of nonquantifiable benefits. For all benefits and costs, note the timing when they will accrue and whether they are one-time or recurring. Capture the assumptions underlying each of the key benefits/costs.

2. There are a number of financial formulas that can be used to evaluate each design, including discounted cash flow (DCF), cost-benefit analysis (CBA), payback period (PB), internal rate of review (IRR), or net present value (NPV). Get agreement ahead of time on the algorithm or calculation behind the financial formula that is selected. When the financial analysis is complete, have a management review session to obtain consensus.

3. The final design alternative decision is best made by blending a number of decision criteria, including risk, to select the final design.

(continued)

Example of Completed Business Case

Years ($Thousands)

	2003	2004	2005	2006	2007	2008	Total
Implementation Costs	($960.48)	($1,199.52)					($2,160.00)
Migration to Shared Services							—
Severance packages		($167.86)	—	—	—	—	($167.86)
Retention bonuses		($120.00)	—	—	—	—	($120.00)
Training	($34.00)	($119.00)	($17.00)	—	—	—	($170.00)
Initial Case Outflows	**($994.48)**	**($1,606.38)**	**($17.00)**	**—**	**—**	**—**	**($2,617.86)**
Technology HW/SW	($192.00)	($288.00)					($480.00)
Ongoing Costs (IS Outsourcing)		($1,000.24)	($1,333.65)	($1,400.34)	($1,470.35)	($1,543.87)	($6,748.45)
Additional Cash Outflow	**($192.00)**	**($1,288.24)**	**($1,350.65)**	**($1,400.34)**	**($1,470.35)**	**($1,543.87)**	**($7,228.45)**
TOTAL INVESTMENT	**($1,186.48)**	**($2,894.62)**	**($1,350.65)**	**($1,400.34)**	**($1,470.35)**	**($1,543.87)**	**($9,846.31)**
Bill-to-cash—FTE Reduction (44-34)		$195.05	$780.22	$819.23	$860.19	$903.20	$3,557.89
Bill-to-cash—Volume Growth Absorption			$43.52	$140.08	$193.12	$236.64	$613.36
Bill-to-cash—Comp Adj Elim (on eliminated employees)		$29.26	$40.96	$43.01	$45.16	$47.42	$205.81
Bill-to-Cash Subtotal		**$244.31**	**$684.70**	**$1,002.32**	**$1,098.47**	**$1,187.26**	**$4,377.06**
Procure-to-Pay—FTE Reduction (22 to 18)		$68.86	$275.45	$289.23	$303.69	$318.87	$1,256.10
Procure-to-Pay—Volume Growth Absorption			$38.62	$77.25	$130.29	$236.64	$482.80
Procure-to-Pay—Comp Adj Elim (on eliminated employees)		$10.33	$14.46	$15.18	$15.94	$16.74	$72.65
Procure-to-Pay—Strategic Sourcing Spend Reduction		$154.20	$1,156.52	$1,542.03	$1,696.23	$1,865.85	$6,414.83
Procure-to-Pay—Subtotal		**$233.39**	**$1,485.05**	**$1,923.69**	**$2,146.15**	**$2,438.10**	**$8,226.38**
IS—FTE Reduction (103 to 95)		$405.73	$540.97	$540.97	$540.97	$540.97	$2,569.61
IS—Comp Adj Elim (on eliminated employees)		$27.05	$28.40	$29.82	$31.31	$32.88	$149.46
IS—Outsourcing (17 FTEs)		$1,333.65	$1,778.21	$1,867.12	$1,960.47	$2,058.50	$8,997.95
IS—Subtotal		**$1,766.43**	**$2,347.58**	**$2,437.91**	**$2,532.75**	**$2,632.35**	**$11,717.02**
Division Office Lease Reduction			—	$38.34	$76.69	$191.72	$306.75
TOTAL BENEFITS		**$2,224.13**	**$4,697.33**	**$5,402.26**	**$5,854.06**	**$6,449.43**	**$24,627.21**
Net Cash Flow (NCF)	($1,186.48)	($670.49)	$3,346.68	$4,001.92	$4,383.71	$4,905.56	$14,780.90
Cumulative NCF	($1,186.48)	($1,856.97)	$1,489.71	$5,491.63	$9,875.34	**$14,780.89**	
Discounted Cash Flow (DCF)	($1,036.23)	($511.42)	$2,229.45	$2,328.34	$2,227.48	$2,176.98	$7,414.50
Cumulative DCF with WACC = 14.50%	($1,036.23)	($1,547.65)	$681.80	$3,010.14	$4,237.62	$7,414.61	
Internal Rate of Return (IRR)							
Payback Period							
Discounted Payback Period							

(continued)

Blank Template

Itemization of Benefits and Costs	2007	2008	2009	2010	2012	Total
I. COSTS						
Infrastructure						
Moving						
Purchase						
Site assessment						
Rent						
Other???						
Infrastructure Subtotal	0	0	0	0	0	0
Outside Vendors						
Consultants						
Other???						
Outside Vendor Subtotal	0	0	0	0	0	0
Organizational						
Severance Packages						
Retention bonuses						
Training						
Other???						
Organizational Subtotal	0	0	0	0	0	0
Technology						
Applications						
Hardware						
Other???						
Technology Subtotal	0	0	0	0	0	0
TOTAL INVESTMENT/COST	0	0	0	0	0	0
II. BENEFITS						
Infrastructure						
Selling of furniture/infrastructure						
Selling real estate						
Site assessment						
Lease reduction						
Other???						
Infrastructure Subtotal	0	0	0	0	0	0
Outside Vendors						
Consultants						
Other???						
Outside Vendor Subtotal	0	0	0	0	0	0
Organizational						
Headcount reduction (compensation)						
Headcount reduction (benefits)						
Training						
Other???						
Organizational Subtotal	0	0	0	0	0	0
Technology						
Applications						
Hardware						
Outsourcing						
Other???						
Technology Subtotal	0	0	0	0	0	0
TOTAL BENEFITS	0	0	0	0	0	0
Cost-Benefit Analysis	#DIV/0!	#DIV/0!	#DIV/0!	#DIV/0!	#DIV/0!	
Payback Period						
Discounted Cash Flow (DCF)						
Internal Rate of Return (IRR)						
Net Present Value (NPV)						

Chartering Template

What is it and when should it be used?

A project charter is a PMO tool that is most commonly used to formalize and clarify a large piece of project-related work. A well-crafted charter will minimally identify the project team members, the objectives or desired outcomes, deliverables, a detailed work plan, and resource requirements or budgeting. When completed, this tool can be combined with an RCI chart to specify team member decision rights.

The chartering template is most commonly used during the Design phase while completing the Organize Project task. If a number of sub-teams or work streams are created, additional charters may be created during subsequent phases of the organization redesign project.

How to do it:

1. Depending on the size/complexity of the design, you may need to break the project into a number of different work streams. It is critical to clarify the key roles of the team, including the sponsor, project leader, and core and ad hoc team members.

2. Identify the performance objectives or desired impacts. These should be translated into both quantitative and qualitative performance targets.

3. Scope creep is one of the most difficult PMO challenges to address. Clarifying specifically what is and is not in scope can be a valuable use of time to keep the team focused on crafting deliverables that are completed on time, within budget, and of acceptable quality.

4. Deliverables are defined as concrete outcomes, *not* activities a project team focuses on that directly impact the desired outcomes or objectives.

5. The next section focuses on developing a detailed work plan. Care should be exercised to appropriately decompose the tasks into activities noting start/end times. For complex projects, it might also be advisable to use more sophisticated functionality like critical path management or PERT to understand the relationships between tasks (predecessors) and provide much more clarity around task responsibility.

6. The final template can be used to forecast capacity and resource requirements that can bubble up to a project budget if desired.

(continued)

Blank Sample Charter

Project/Work Stream	

Objectives

1. _____
2. _____
3. _____

Scope of Work

Included in the Scope	Excluded from the Scope
•	
•	
•	
•	
•	
•	
•	
•	
•	
•	

Deliverables

1. _____
2. _____
3. _____

(continued)

Chartering Template *(continued)*

Major Steps	Week Starting:																					
	12-May	26-May	9-Jun	23-Jun	7-Jul	21-Jul	4-Aug	18-Aug	1-Sep	15-Sep	29-Sep	13-Oct	27-Oct	10-Nov	24-Nov	8-Dec	22-Dec					

(continued)

Resource Requirements

Item	Q 1/07	Q 2/07	Q 3/07	Q 4/07	2007	Project Total
			Period			
Team Members	Days by Period					
Contractor(s)						
Consultant(s)						
Resources Days Subtotal	0	0	0	0	0	0
Project Cost Summary	Dollars by Period					
Employees	0	0	0	0	0	0
Consultants and Contractors	0	0	0	0	0	0
Travel and Entertainment	0	0	0	0		0
Capital Item Depreciation	0	0	0	0		0
Training and Education						0
Other						0
Project Cost Subtotal	$0	$0	$0	$0	$0	$0
Capital Expenditures	Dollars by Period					
						0
						0
						0
Capital Expenditures Subtotal	$0	$0	$0	$0	$0	$0
Savings/Revenue Increases	Dollars by Period					
Not Estimated	0					0
	0					0
						0
						0
	0					0
Saving/Revenue Subtotal	$0	$0	$0	$0	$0	$0
Net Present Value	N/A					

(continued)

Completed Example

Project/Work Stream	Improve Disbursements Payment Process	
Sponsor	Michael Douglas	
Project Leader	Michael Pagani	
Team Members Core	Ahmad Rashad	Fay Ray
	Tiki Barger	
	Mario Puzzo	
Ad Hoc	Joe Torre	

Objectives

1. Shorten disbursement payment cycle time by 35%.*
2. Reduce invoicing errors to 1%.*
3. Improve internal and external customer satisfaction.*

*Some of the above numbers to be finalized later in the work plan.

(continued)

Scope of Work

Included in the Scope	Excluded in the Scope
• Contract processing and payment	• Receiving activities
• Processing miscellaneous payments	•
• Processing PO payments	
• Document scanning and records management	
• Competency and skill requirements definition	•
• Organization and job design for AP	•
• Maintenance of vendor records	
• Invoice receipt	
• Handle vendor payment inquiries/problems	
• Activities to ensure contract payment compliance	

Deliverables

1. A/P process design documentation
2. Procedure documentation (if different than above)
3. Audit of implementation effectiveness
4. Performance measurement reports

(continued)

Chartering Template *(continued)*

Major Steps	Week Starting:										
	20-Jan	03-Feb	17-Feb	03-Mar	17-Mar	31-Mar	14-Apr	28-Apr	12-May	26-May	09-Jun
1. Review and agree on charter with team.	▓										
2. Provide team with some process management methodology training (if no ongoing coaching).	▓	▓							▓	▓	
3. Complete "as-is" level 1 AP process stream definition for contract and PO payments.	▓	▓	▓								
4. Define "as-is" process to level 2/3 and match responsibilities to the organization structure.											
PO payments											
Miscellaneous payments											
Contract payments											
5. Identify and define any regulatory or other business rules that constrain process design.											
6. Design and implement initial measurements to establish baseline.											
7. Confirm/detail objectives (if needed).											
8. Detail agreed "to-be" A/P processes to level 2/3 (based on pre-agreed and documented changes).											
PO payments											
Miscellaneous payments											
Contract payments											
9. Finalize Oracle solution configuration.											
10. Document skill requirements for "to-be" process.											
11. Define volume and workload requirements and preliminary staffing.											
12. Define organization structure alternatives with sponsor and decide.											
13 Finalize organization design and develop job descriptions.											
14. Develop organization change implementation plan.											
15. Communicate and facilitate reorganization.											
16 Develop and deliver implementation training (inclusive of procedures).											
Develop and deliver Oracle training.											
Develop and deliver process training.											

(continued)

Resource Requirements

Item	Period					Project Total
	Q 1/07	Q 2/07	Q 3/07	Q 4/07	2007	
Team Members	Days by Period					
Michael Pagani	10	30	20	10		70
Ahmand Rashad	8	24	16	8		56
Tiki Barber	8	24	16	8		56
Mario Puzzo	8	24	16	8		56
						0
						0
Contractor(s)						0
Consultant(s)						0
Resources Days Subtotal	34	102	68	34	0	238
Project Cost Summary	Dollars by Period					
Employees	17	51	34	17	0	119
Consultants and Contractors	0	0	0	0	0	0
Travel and Entertainment						0
Capital Item Depreciation	0	0	0	0		0
Training and Education						0
Other						0
Project Cost Subtotal	$17	$51	$34	$17	$0	$119
Capital Expenditures	Dollars by Period					
						0
						0
						0
Capital Expenditures Subtotal	$0	$0	$0	$0	$0	$0
Savings/Revenue Increases	Dollars by Period					
Not Estimated						0
						0
						0
						0
Saving/Revenue Subtotal	$0	$0	$0	$0	$0	$0
Net Present Value	N/A					

Coordinating Mechanisms Template

What is it and when should it be used?

A coordinating mechanism is a discrete set of actions that are designed to optimize how interdependent units work together.

This tool is one of the most complex within the organization design toolkit. Because of the difficulty, it is recommended that you identify and partner with a person who is thoroughly experienced in organization design.

The coordinating mechanisms template should be used to identify and design specific actions for interdependent units to work together effectively after the design changes have been implemented. Coordinating mechanisms will allow you to do the following:

- Better identify the information/data work units needed to deliver their core product/service
- Improve inter-unit communications and collaboration
- Align core processes cross-functionally
- Reduce role ambiguity
- Surface and resolve conflict

This tool should be used during the Design phase when completing Detailed Design.

How to do it:

There are two distinct options for identifying coordinating mechanisms: the "quick and dirty" and "full" approaches. The "quick and dirty" approach is most suitable for simple design projects that encompass few locations and only include two to three distinct functions. The "full" approach is for enterprise-wide projects. Listed below are the steps for completing each approach:

I. Quick and Dirty Approach

1. **Identify unit interdependencies.** Identify the interdependencies between all the units within the scope of the project. Prioritize the interdependencies based on how critical each interdependency is to organizational performance.

2. **Identify historical problems.** If the units have historically been interdependent, identify "fumbles" that have occurred where work has been handed off from one unit to another. This typically occurs at boundaries between work units.

3. **Understand "new" interdependencies.** Organization redesign often incorporates process redesign. It is important to map out and understand in detail how information flows across work processes and the new structure.

4. **Brainstorm coordinating mechanisms.** When there have been historical interdependencies, identify problems that have occurred, prioritize them, understand the root cause, and develop targeted coordinating mechanisms to address the most critical historical problem areas. For new interdependencies, brainstorm the most likely "derailers" and identify coordinating methods to eliminate/reduce problem areas.

(continued)

5. **Engage appropriate stakeholders.** Since coordinating mechanisms by their definition involve more than one unit, it is imperative to involve stakeholders from the other unit as early in the process as possible. This will enhance the identification of problems, root cause, derailers, and ultimately the adoption of coordinating mechanisms. See the example below of a completed coordinating mechanism template for a sales function within a software company:

Historical Problem Areas	Root Cause	Coordinating Mechanism
Client relationship managers (CRMs) don't cross sell our services	Get involved too late in the sales process to have our services included in the RFP	When leads are identified, our group will assist in writing **all** proposals to incorporate our services as needed
Low client satisfaction with the delivery of our consulting services	CRMs do not solicit any client feedback on our services since they are not part of the foundation of our service offerings	Develop a pulse survey that CRMs will administer at the end of each project phase. Data will be analyzed to improve service delivery.

II. Full Approach

1. The first step is to understand the decision rights using an RCI chart. An RCI chart identifies who is **R**esponsible (R) for completing each activity, who must be **C**onsulted (C), and who must be **I**nformed (I) of the activity. Information for an RCI chart is most commonly generated as follows:

   - **Straw man exercise:** A person or small group develops a working draft for a larger group of stakeholders to respond to.
   - **White board exercise:** A workshop is conducted for a group of people to assign the R, C, I "real time."
   - **Survey feedback:** A survey is administered to a group, whose feedback is used to assign R, C, and I based on where the letters were most commonly positioned.

2. It may be clearer to think in terms of an organization chart as the R, C, and I are assigned. This will help ensure that the functions/roles are connected to the items listed in the left column. Use the chart (see example on the next page) to plot the processes/activities/decisions to the function/role, assigning an R, C, or I to the cells. A letter does not have to be assigned to every cell. It is possible for more than one function/role to be consulted/informed for an activity, but only one function can be responsible for an activity.

(continued)

RCI Chart Example

Activities/Decisions	Function/Role 1	Function/Role 2	Function/Role 3	Function/Role 4				
Activity 1	R	I	I	C				
Activity 2	C	I	R	I				
Activity 3	R	C	C	I				
Activity 4	C	I	C	R				
Activity 5	C	R	C	C				
Activity 6	I	C	I	R				

3. If the RCI chart looks too complex after completing, with multiple letters assigned to many cells, this means that the process could be too complicated. If this is the case, consider reassigning letters or removing letters from the template (The Responsibility and Consulting designations are the most important).

4. Determine the coordinating mechanisms that must be incorporated into the future state design by using the Identify Coordinating Mechanisms table. The table can be used to identify the most appropriate type of coordinating mechanism. Listed below are the steps:

- **Importance.** Assess the importance of each interdependency by determining how critical it is to the organization.
- **Complexity.** Assess how complex the interactions are. Greater complexity requires more sophisticated methods of coordination.
- **Task uncertainty.** How well defined are the task and activities in the process. Rules are more sufficient for predictable and repeatable activities. Liaison roles are more appropriate when there is greater ambiguity and unpredictability on the outcomes for the activities. These require more interdependence and sharing of outcomes and need to be timelier. The scale for assessing Task Uncertainty is 1 for Predictable repeatable task and 10 for more Ambiguous and Unpredictable.
- **Interdependence.** This refers to the level and type of interdependence between groups and activities. The scale for assessing interdependence is 1 for Pooled interdependence, 5 for Sequential interdependence, and 10 for Reciprocal interdependence. There are generally three different kinds of interdependence, each requiring different types of coordinating mechanisms:
  - **Reciprocal.** Certain outputs of each group become an input for the other group. Collaboration needs to occur in both directions (e.g., R & D, market research).
  - **Sequential.** Outputs of one group become the input of the other group (e.g., manufacturing and shipping departments).
  - **Pooled.** Groups are relatively independent of each other, but contribute to the overall goals of the organization (e.g., holding company).

(continued)

5. One can interpret the Identify Coordinating Mechanisms table as follows: Typically the majority of your decision criteria will cluster toward the top one-third, middle one-third, or lower one-third of the table. If they cluster around the top, then coordinating mechanisms such as rules, formal hierarchy, etc., are most appropriate. Conversely, if the majority of the decision criteria cluster around the bottom of the table, then more complex coordinating methods would be appropriate (e.g., lateral processes, integrator roles). Listed below is a brief description of the most common coordinating methods:

- **Rules, programs, procedures.** Specific examples of coordinating mechanisms include developing SOPs, policies, or rules for problem resolution and practices that specify the desired behaviors, govern decision making, and/or limit discretion in advance.

- **Formal hierarchy.** Examples include appointing a common manager to oversee two different units, holding regular meetings to coordinate activities, or using Centers of Excellence to ensure alignment. Other examples may be to have overlapping membership across interdependent units or use shared services functionality.

- **Targets/Goals.** This can include specifying outputs, goals, or targets to coordinate interdependent groups.

- **Networks.** There are many networks that include formal or informal vehicles for encouraging knowledge sharing across functions, businesses, and geographies. There are six common ways to foster networks: co-location, communities of practice (i.e., groups of employees that share common organizational interests), annual meetings/retreats, training programs, rotational assignments, and technology/ e-coordination (e.g., chat groups, Web sites, e-mail distribution lists on intranet, Lotus Notes, Microsoft Exchange, instant messaging, group calendar management, shared databases).

- **Liaison roles.** There are a myriad of ways to use a liaison as a channel to align interdependent functions. Typically, individuals in these roles serve as a source of information and expertise to advise a work group. Rarely do they have formal authority; the liaison position is usually part-time.

- **Teams.** There are a number of different team configurations across a conceptual continuum from issue teams, cross-functional teams, steering teams, and task forces to self-directed work groups. Teams can either be permanent or ad hoc, but their value is in pooling expertise, breaking down functional silos, and coordinating efforts of interdependent units. Some teams use SLAs or partnership agreements to facilitate cross-unit cooperation.

- **Lateral processes.** These are the three to five processes that are mission critical and cut across multiple functions within the organization. These processes should be mapped and include metrics at the end of the process, where the process crosses functions, and where performance problems have occurred historically.

- **Integrator roles.** There are three common types of integrator roles: **managerial** (an individual who is responsible for taking a general management point of view in helping multiple work groups accomplish a joint task such as a project, brand, program, or account manager), **process owner** (an individual who is typically responsible for all of the activities within a process from cradle to grave), or **boundary-spanning** positions (i.e., chief learning officer) that ensure that the work of each unit is aligned with the business strategy.

(continued)

Identify Coordinating Mechanisms Table

Units	Importance	Complexity	Task Uncertainty	Interdependence	Types of Integrating Methods
	1 ↕ 10	Low ↕ High	Low ↕ High	Pooled ↕ Sequential ↕ Reciprocal	Rules, programs, procedures Formal hierarchy Targets/goals Networks Liaison roles Teams Lateral processes Integrator roles

Example of a Completed Coordinating Mechanisms Table

Internal Units	Importance	Complexity	Task Uncertainty	Interdependence	Types of Integrating Methods
Implementations	3	2	2	3	Create standard operating procedures to align work units
DSR Team	9	3	2	5	Create a scorecard that incents both units to work together and align the efforts of both groups
Sales	8	5	7	8	Establish a cross-functional team
Data Conversion	9	9	8	8	Establish a process owner who has responsibility from cradle to grave

Design Alternative Decision Matrix

What is it and when should it be used?

This tool is most commonly used during the Design phase when completing the Macro and Detailed Design. It can be used to prioritize and ultimately select the best design alternative via a structured process using objective decision criteria. This tool can be used in conjunction with the business case and risk assessment tools to compare and contrast the financial impacts of each design alternative.

How to do it:

1. When identifying design alternatives, try to pare down your alternatives to no more than four different design options.

2. Listed below are the commonly used decision criteria:
   — The design metrics
   — The design principles
   — The degree to which existing problems/weaknesses with the current structure are designed out
   — Degree to which desired functionality is delivered
   — Risk and/or financial return

   Experience suggests that you use no more than three different categories (e.g., design principles, design metrics) of decision criteria or you risk overwhelming the design team with too much choice.

3. Identify a qualitative (H, M, L) or quantitative scale to evaluate each design alternative against decision criteria. Pick the design alternative that provides the best benefits vis-à-vis the criteria.

(continued)

Design Alternative Decision Matrix *(continued)*

Example of a Completed Tool

Design Alternatives	Direction	Design Principles				Problem/Desired Functionality			Return		Total
	Fit with Design Vision	Strategy drives the redesign	Aggressively apply enabling technology	Outsource non-strategic functions	Optimize processes cross-functionally	Not aligned to VOC	Decision making too centralized	Slow response to envelope changes	Risk analysis	Financial analysis	
Design change 1	3	2	1	3	2	3	3	3	3	3	26
Design change 2	1	2	2	2	3	2	2	1	2	1	18
Design change 3	2	1	3	1	2	2	1	1	1	1	15
Design change 4	1	1	1	1	2	1	3	1	3	1	15

Key: (For risk analysis invert key)		
High = 4	Medium = 3	Low =2

(continued)

Organization Design: A Practical Methodology and Toolkit

Example of a Blank Tool

Design Alternatives	Direction	Design Principles				Problem/Desired Functionality			Return		Total

Design/Implementation Challenge Questions

What is it and when should it be used?

The challenge questions can be used to provide an objective sanity check regarding the future state organization structure. It can be used to ensure that the desired functionality has been fully designed into the new structure and to identify and foster discussion around a myriad of implementation issues.

This tool should be used during the Design phase when completing the Macro and Detailed Design activities.

How to do it:

Listed below are some questions that you may selectively use to complete a challenge session:

1. To what extent does the proposed structure closely support the business strategy?
2. Does the structure meet the vision, design principles, and quantified redesign objectives?
   - Have the suppliers, customers, inputs, and outputs been sufficiently documented to operationalize the new structure?
   - Has duplicate functionality (e.g., multiple units that provide training) been minimized across the structure?
   - Are the roles and responsibilities clearly delineated?
3. Does the structure achieve the desired functionality and is it aligned to the key core and support processes?
4. Does the proposed structure still incorporate the strengths from the current structure but minimize/eliminate key structural weaknesses?
5. Have you identified the new competencies that are required to successfully execute the new structure?
6. Has the "short list" of alternative designs been subjected to risk and financial analysis?
7. Have you identified the specific technology changes that must be implemented to support the new structure?
8. Does the new structure/process minimize non-value-added work?
9. Do you fully understand the effect the proposed structural changes will have on your existing facilities' asset base?
   - Number/location of facilities
   - Physical layout

(continued)

10. Do we have the right people doing the right work?

11. Have policies and business rules been updated to tightly align to the new structure?

12. Does the new structure require cultural changes? What specific behaviors and norms need to be enhanced or reduced?

13. Have the appropriate HR practices been modified to support the new structure?
    - Career ladder
    - Recruiting
    - Performance metrics
    - Rewards/recognition
    - Performance management

14. Have you addressed all of the coordinating mechanisms needed to ensure that inter-dependent units work effectively together?

15. For each function/department:
    - Are spans of control optimal?
    - Are the number of layers optimal?
    - Are the activities performed in each unit consistent with its mission?
    - Have the information flows been mapped?
    - Do the products/services of each unit add value?

Design Principles/Metrics Template

What is it and when should it be used?

Design principles are general parameters that guide the design of the organization from selection of the high-level structure to designing roles and jobs. Design principles typically cascade from the business strategy and a vision statement (if used), which describes what the future state organization structure will look like.

Once the design principles have been finalized, they must be translated into a short list of metrics that can be used to assist in prioritizing design alternatives and later on to evaluate the effectiveness of the implemented design.

This tool should be used during the Define phase when completing the Establish Design Parameters step.

How to do it:

1. Brainstorm a list of design principles using the business strategy, voice of the customer data, available best practices, and future state organization design vision (if available). From the business strategy, make sure you fully understand how opportunities, threats, and key business challenges are likely to impact the organization structure.

2. Prioritize the list by identifying the "nice to haves" and then selecting the high impact "must haves" principles (the final list should be no more than eight principles).

3. Translate the design principles into a list of five or fewer qualitative and quantitative design metrics.

(continued)

Completed Example of a Design Principles and Design Metrics Template

Design Principles	Design Metrics
• Strategy and the future state processes drive the redesign	• No more than four layers between president and lowest level in the organization
• Outsource nonstrategic functionality	• Reduce the cycle times of key processes by at least 30%
• Optimize processes cross-functionally	• Realize an average span of control of 1:8
• Aggressively apply enabling technology	• Reduce headcount by 15%
• Leadership Competency Model will be utilized in job definition	• Reduce operating costs by 20%
	• Final design will be cost neutral

Blank Design Principles and Design Metrics Template

Design Principles	Design Metrics
•	•
•	•
•	•
•	•
•	•
•	•

Employee Selection Guidelines

What is it and when should it be used?

The purpose of this tool is to provide an approach to select employees for roles in the new organization. If the redesign includes an enterprise-wide scope, it is not uncommon for selection to occur hierarchically top-down (level 1, 2, 3, etc.) and in different time intervals. As each level of leader is selected, he or she typically selects his or her direct reports.

The selection process should be fully designed during the Design phase and will be executed during the Implement phase.

How to do it:

The following principles should be followed when completing this activity:

- **Objectivity.** Selection decisions should be made based on objective observations.

- **A sense of urgency.** Complete the process as quickly as possible. The longer the process, the higher the employee angst and the greater the likelihood that you will experience involuntary loss of key talent.

- **Full participation.** All members of the selection team should participate in the discussions.

- **Evidence based.** Decisions should be based on thorough and accurate information.

- **Transparency and understandability.** Communicate the process to employees so that they understand how selection decisions were made. When interfacing with employees, always demonstrate respect.

- **Skill/behavior driven.** Decisions should be made based on the leadership, technical, and functional skills and behaviors required for successful performance on the specific job.

- **Open dialogue.** Discussions about selection should be open, honest, and direct.

The selection team should have broad leadership representation, including HR, and a discussion is expected to accompany each decision. The objective for these discussions is to ensure that the right employees are selected when considering the skills required for the role and the requirements of the business.

Listed below are general selection steps that most organizations can follow:

1. **Identify future state roles and critical requirements.** Initially the focus should be on identifying the characteristics of all roles in the organization. This should include the job title, job description with expected activities associated with the position, level, location, number of positions, and other related organizational information. Care should be exercised in determining the technical skills (skills required to get the job done) and behavioral skills (skills needed to build the organization for the future).

(continued)

2. **Identify a slate of candidates.** A slate is the group of employees to be considered for positions associated with a role. It is important to recognize that only employees included on a slate will be assessed against the role success factors and potentially selected to one of the associated positions. The documentation of characteristics and skills completed in the last step provides baseline data for determining which employees should be included on a slate, such as

   - role skill requirements;
   - location of the role;
   - level of the role; and
   - number of position associated with the role.

3. **Evaluate candidates.** Use consistent and job-related criteria to evaluate each individual on the slate. Refer to any relevant employee data (succession planning data, past performance appraisals, 360° assessments) to assist in the final decision. Listed below are some general guidelines:

   - **Experience.** The assessment/selection team must have experience observing the employee's performance of the skills required by the role.
   - **Consistent quality.** Each assessment should undergo multiple levels of review to remove bias and promote a consistent quality of assessment.
   - **Fairness.** The assessment process needs to be fair and equitable. Each employee on a slate will be assessed only against the skills assigned to the role. The result of each employee assessment will be numerical scores and qualitative data representing the demonstration of each skill. Each employee assessment will go through a series of reviews before being provided to the selection team for consideration of roles in the new organization.
   - **Best decisions/no bias.** A review of employee assessments not only promotes the selection of the most skilled employees, but it seeks to remove the existence or appearance of bias in assessment decisions.

Develop a template to consistently evaluate each candidate.

(continued)

Sample Rating Template

Rating	Rating Scale	Definition
3	High Match	Clearly and consistently both exceeds objectives and demonstrates exceptional accomplishments Sought after for his or her skills, expertise, and results Recognized as exceptional by others—both within and outside his or her group
2	Match	Achieves objectives and demonstrates competency in critical performance dimensions Meets high standards of performance and, at times, may go beyond acceptable but demanding performance standards Recognized as adding value, especially in key areas of responsibility
1	Not a Match	Achieves some, but not all, objectives of the job with a reasonable degree of proficiency Need for further development and improvement is clearly recognized by his or her management Improvement in performance is required

4. **Finalize selections.** Before finalizing selections, you should solicit the input of both your Human Resources and Legal staff to ensure that you are not exposing your organization to litigation (e.g., wrongful discharge suits, adverse impact).

Function/Process Relationship Mapping

What is it and when should it be used?

Function/process relationship maps are tools that can be used to quickly understand how work gets done across an enterprise-wide level. It can be used to

- understand at a macro level the key inputs/outputs between internal/external suppliers and customers;
- visualize the relationship (inputs/outputs) between individual processes/functions;
- identify performance problems;
- specify functional relationships.

When using this tool, it is critical to remember that the documentation process is iterative; since you are trying to get a high level "snapshot," you must focus on key inputs/outputs only and use stakeholders to verify accuracy of data. Additional data to potentially include on the maps are structural/process problems, their root cause, potential remedies, as well as desired performance characteristics.

This tool is introduced during the Define phase when Assessing the Current State.

How to do it:

Listed below are the steps for creating a functional relationship map:

1. Select a level of analysis (function/department) and be consistent throughout the map.
   - Level 1: Function
   - Level 2: Department
2. Identify all the functions/departments that are within scope of the analysis.
3. Draw and label a box on the right edge of the page for customers. Draw and label a box for each function/department.
4. Starting with customers and working backward, identify the key inputs and outputs between each function/department. Draw arrows to illustrate the direction of the relationship and label each arrow.
5. Continue documentation until you have worked back to the supplier's box located on the left side of the page opposite customers.

Listed below are the steps for creating a process relationship map:

1. Create a box and label it "Customers."
2. Identify key organizational outputs.
3. Identify the organization's key processes. Create a separate box for each process.
4. Identify the inputs/outputs for each process.
5. Work from right to left, starting with "Customers." Draw arrows between each process to identify input/output interfaces.
6. Work backward until you have identified all the input/output interfaces between customers and suppliers.

(continued)

Example of Completed Function Relationship Map

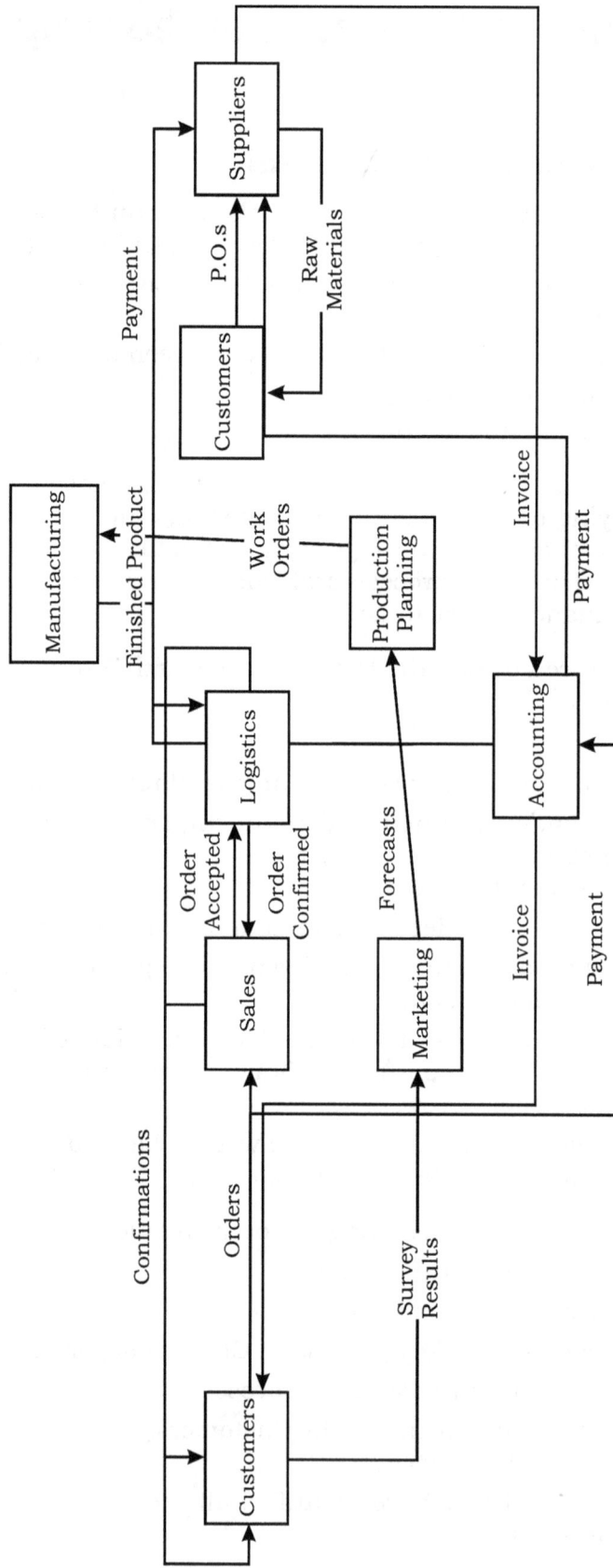

(continued)

Example of Completed Process Relationship Map

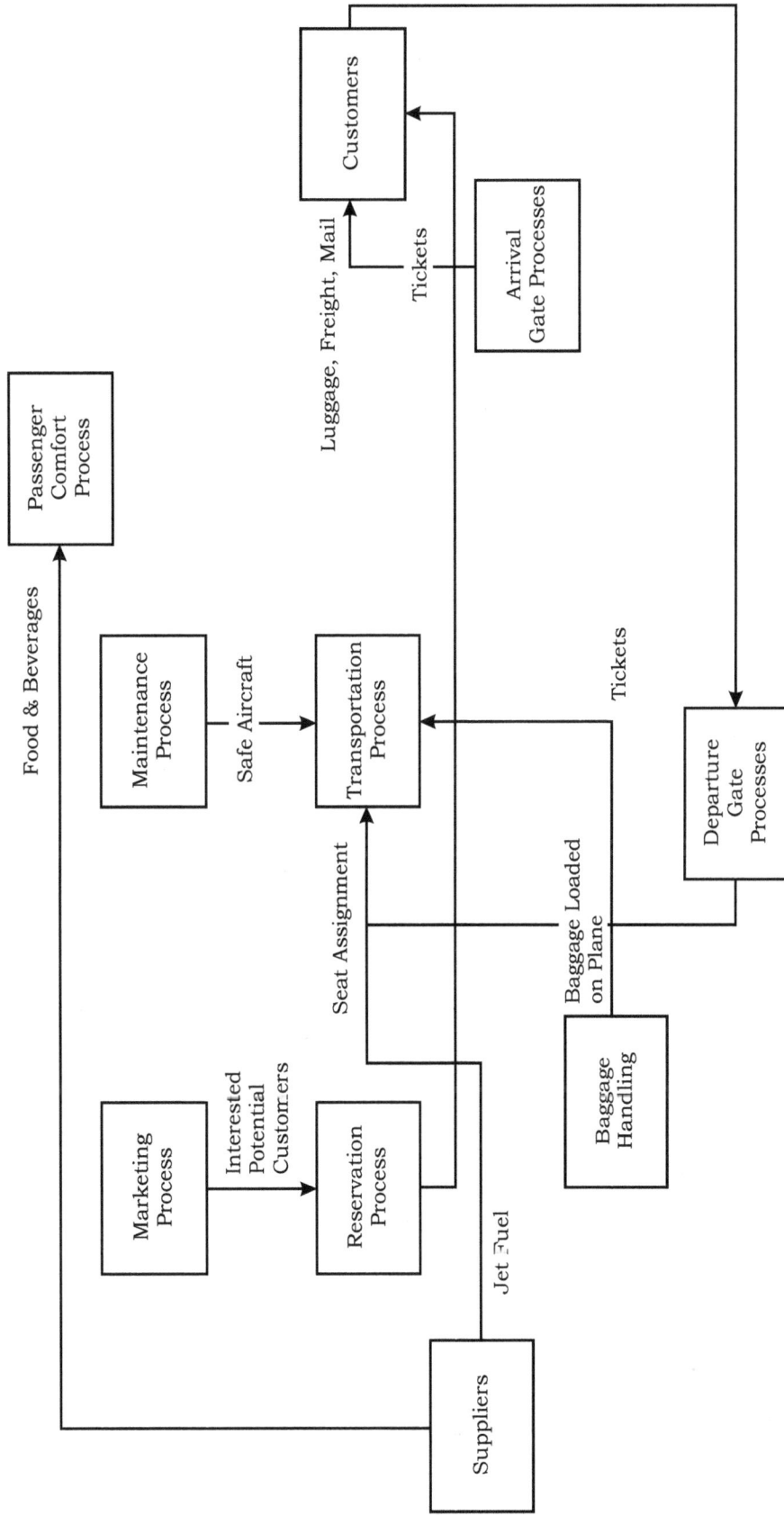

Human Capital Redeployment Primer

I. **Benefits of HC Redeployment**
   - Can provide a win-win outcome for both the organization and employees
   - Decreases costs associated with hiring and training of new employees
   - Reduces severance costs
   - Leverages knowledge management and retains organizational memory
   - Enhances employee perceptions and loyalty
   - Maintains employee morale and company image

II. **Common Types of Redeployment Services Offered**
   - **Emotional assistance:** Aiding employees with the psychological effects of transition
   - **Job posting:** Using an internal job-bidding system
   - **Sponsorship:** Asking other parts of the organization to find appropriate employment opportunities
   - **Résumé book:** Providing an electronic or paper summary of the qualifications of all displaced employees
   - **Retraining:** Providing company-paid training to enhance the skill levels of employees
   - **Testing:** Offering job-interest testing and psychological and skill evaluations

III. **Common Types of Redeployment Options**
   - **Job redesign**
     - Enrichment
   - **Outplacement**
     - Counseling services
     - Transition centers
     - Job-search training
     - Networking
     - Résumé preparation
     - Clerical support
   - **Increase legitimate needs for workers**
     - Accelerate capital-type projects
     - Bring in outsourced functionality
   - **Job banks**
   - **Retraining programs**
   - **Redeployment**
     - Use internal skills for special projects
   - **Liberalize use of unpaid absence**
     - Sabbaticals
   - **Terminate**
   - **Accelerate natural attrition**
     - Increase early retirement benefits
     - Lower minimum retirement age
     - Offer early retirement package
   - **Institute "up or out" programs**
   - **Stimulate creation of more jobs in local community**
   - **Provide post-retirement "consulting" arrangements**
   - **Loan to government or community organizations**

Impact Analysis Template

What is it and when should it be used?

This tool can be used to proactively identify how any proposed organization design changes will impact the organization.

All organizations, whether they be Fortune 500 conglomerates or "mom and pop" family companies, have an architecture that comprises three distinct elements: **T**echnology, **O**rganization, and **P**rocess. Technology comprises the data employees need to make decisions, the information systems hardware (telephony, servers, PCs, etc.), the production/operations technology that is instrumental in delivering your core product/service, and the software applications that interface with process and hardware. The organization comprises the administrative policies or business rules that drive behavior, business systems (e.g., planning, budgeting), human resource practices (everything from recruiting and rewards to succession planning), capabilities, workforce competencies, and the organization structure (job design, reporting relationships, staffing levels). And lastly, the process element comprises the business processes, physical infrastructure of the business (the site strategy—number and location of work locations), and physical layout of work areas (the arrangement of offices, conference rooms, etc.). The value of this tool is that it will allow you to proactively identify the specific "ripple effects" of any design changes to both minimize the time needed for implementation and optimize the potential for success.

The impact analysis tool is most commonly used during the Design phase when completing Macro or Detailed Design or during the Implementation phase.

How to do it:

1. **Complete the Understanding Impacts to Business Architecture Matrix.** This matrix can be used to facilitate discussions around the likely impacts any design changes will have on each element of architecture. Make sure you spend sufficient time vetting each element of architecture. This matrix can be used to ensure that your future state organization design solution addresses all of the necessary change management elements.

2. **Complete the Understanding Impacts to External Stakeholders Matrix.** This matrix is applicable if a stakeholder assessment has not been completed earlier. It will identify all key stakeholders, ensure that the impacts of the design changes are fully understood and that the solution has effectively addressed all key stakeholder impacts/concerns.

3. **Integrate learnings into the transition plan.** A well-crafted organization design project uses a discovery process. The completion of each tool provides an output that ultimately becomes an input to some other activity (risk management, communications, stakeholder engagement) downstream.

(continued)

Step 1: Understanding Impacts to Business Architecture

Technology Architecture	Description of Impact	Criticality
• **Applications**		
• **Data**		
• **Hardware**		
• **Production technology**		

Organization Architecture	Description of Impact	Criticality
• **HR practices**		
• **Competencies**		
• **Structure**		
• **Management systems**		
• **Business rules/policies**		

(continued)

Step 1: Understanding Impacts to Business Architecture *(concluded)*

Process Architecture	Description of Impact	Criticality
• **Processes**		
• **Facilities**		
• **Physical layout**		

Step 2: Understanding Impacts to External Stakeholders

Stakeholder Group	Description of Impact	Criticality
• **Customers**		
• **Suppliers/vendors**		
• **Other?**		

(continued)

Sample Completed Organization Impact Assessment by Category

Technology Architecture	Description of Impact	Criticality
• **Applications**	• Retirement of legacy systems to SAP • Centralization of customer related credit risk	H
• **Data**	• Need to create relational databases	L
• **Hardware**	• None	
• **Production technology**	• None	
Organization Architecture	**Description of Impact**	**Criticality**
• **HR practices**	• Align rewards and recognition programs to drive desired behaviors • Modify performance management process	H M
• **Competencies**	• Major job redesign will create major competency gaps relating to the following areas: Analyst will need to learn new data entry application and supervisors will need to develop skills in process improvement.	M
• **Structure**	• Outsource market research functionality	H
• **Business rules/policies**	• Need to change the following policies	M

(continued)

Sample Completed Organization Impact Assessment by Category *(concluded)*

Process Architecture	Description of Impact	Criticality
• **Processes**	• Streamlined credit, claims, and collections processes across the organization • Added customer self-service capabilities • Increased automation of processes and status/actions tracking • Centralized issuing of adjustment	M
• **Facilities**	• Need to close office in New York City • Need to close warehouse in Atlanta	H H
• **Physical layout**	• Redesign layout in corporate headquarters to better utilize team concept	M
Stakeholder Group	**Description of Impact**	**Criticality**
• **Customers**	• Decreased response time to customer inquiries • Increased capability for audit trail	H
• **Suppliers/vendors**	• Expect 50% reduction in ray material suppliers	H
• **Other?**		

Position Profile

What is it and when should it be used?

A position profile documents the key elements of each job within the new organization. Position profiles can be used to communicate the key components of each job and the career ladder or path, and can ultimately be used in recruiting and selection. They should enable employees to understand their relationships to others in the organization and how to perform their jobs successfully.

Depending on the ultimate use of the document, these profiles commonly document the following components for each job:

- Position description statement
- Responsibilities
- Individual performance metrics
- Reporting relationships
- Customers/Contacts
- Potential career paths
- Professional and functional competencies
- Proficiency level for each competency

This template is most commonly used in the Design phase during Detailed Design.

How to do it:

1. Check to see if your organization already has position descriptions for each job. If so, confirm what decisions you intend to make using the position profiles as inputs and modify the format accordingly.

2. Identify any relevant job or process documentation (e.g., completed RCI diagrams, completed role-to-job mapping templates, process maps, old job descriptions) that can serve as an input into the updating of each profile.

3. Develop drafts of each profile and share them with appropriate stakeholders. This can include job incumbents, supervisors, business partners, and customers to fine tune the content.

4. Use the new profiles for key HR activities associated with the new redesign such as recruiting, performance management, and retention.

(continued)

Example of a Completed Position Profile

Position:	Director, Organization Effectiveness
Description:	Provide thought leadership, coaching, codification of methodologies/tools, consulting support, and education to line executives, HR partners, and intact project teams.

Responsibilities:	**Competencies and Attributes:**
• Develop and codify methodologies, tools, and templates to transfer knowledge to key stakeholders • Manage division-wide projects • Provide consulting support in the areas of change management, organization design, and strategy development/deployment • Develop and facilitate needed education • Develop coalitions and cross-functional relationships to leverage intellectual capital • Develop a best practices database to capture learnings from past and ongoing projects	• Strategic thinking (I) • Communications oral, written, listening (I) • Organization design (E) • Strategic planning (E) • Change management (E) • Relationship management (I) • Influencing (I) • Industry knowledge (B) • Decision making (I) • Conceptual thinking (I) • Ability to manage multiple tasks (I) **Key:** (B)=Basic level (I)= Intermediate level (E)=Expert level
Reporting:	**Interfaces/Customers:**
• Reports directly to the GM of business unit • Indirect reporting to the corporate EVP of HR and the divisional VP of HR	• GM/Presidents of each business • Corporate EVP of HR • Division VP of HR • Project teams
Individual Performance Metrics:	**Potential Career Paths:**
• Customer satisfaction • Project effectiveness (on time/on budget) • Project impact (% of project targets realized) • HR partner satisfaction	• Division Vice President, Human Resources • Executive Director, Organization Effectiveness • AVP, Training and Development

(continued)

Blank Position Profile

Position: Description:	
Responsibilities:	**Competencies and Attributes:** **Key:** (B)=Basic level (I)= Intermediate level (E)=Expert level
Reporting:	**Interfaces/Customers:**
Individual Performance Metrics:	**Potential Career Paths:**

RCI Template

What is it and when should it be used?

This tool can be used to clarify responsibility for key decisions and activities. It is most commonly used to clarify roles, responsibilities, and decision-making levels for the project team during the Organize the Project Activity of the Define phase. It is also used during the Design phase when completing the Detailed Design. During this later application, it is centered on clarifying the "decision rights" around roles within the future state structure.

How to do it:

1. Identify the key activities, responsibilities, or decisions that you would like to incorporate into this tool and insert them in column one of the matrix.

2. In the subsequent columns, list the key stakeholders who are likely to be involved.

3. For each key activity, responsibility, or decision, identify

   - who is Responsible for making the final decision or completing the activity;
   - who needs to be Consulted (either before the final decision is made or to get input);
   - who needs to be Informed after the decision is made.

(continued)

Example of a Blank RCI Template

Activities/Responsibilities	Roles/People/Groups							

Key:
Responsibility = R   **Consult = C**   **Inform = I**

(continued)

Example of a Completed RCI Template

Activities/Responsibilities	Roles/People/Groups							
	J. Dean	M. Monroe	F. Williamson	J. Lennon	T. Lilly	M. Harmon	T. Selleck	
Finalize specs	R	C	C	I	I	I	I	
Develop sourcing strategy	C	I	R	I	C	I	C	
Complete initial review of candidates	I	I	I	C	R	C	C	
Select candidate	I	I	I	I	C	R	C	
Negotiate terms	C	R	C	I	I	C	I	
On board	I	I	C	I	C	I	R	

Key:
Responsibility = R   Consult = C   Inform = I

Risk Analysis Tool

What is it and when should it be used?

One of the key success factors in organizational design is the early identification and prioritization of risks. This tool is used to either *eliminate* the most critical risks or *reduce their negative impact* on the success of the organizational design initiative.

This tool should be first used during the Define phase when completing Assess Current State. Risk management is best implemented via a "discovery" process where the plan is periodically updated and executed throughout the project's life cycle. Learnings from the risk management plan should be integrated into the overall project, engagement, and communication plans.

How to do it:

1. Collect archival data and data from a variety of impacted stakeholders to identify the risks to the project.

2. Organize the risks according to themes (organization risks, technology risks, process risks, leadership, etc.).

3. Obtain consensus on the probability of occurrence of each risk.

4. Understand the impact the risk will have on both the organization and the project.

5. Generally, it is a good idea to focus on the risks with the greatest probability of occurrence and largest impact on the project. Fully discuss and then agree on some targeted actions that will either eliminate the risk or minimize its negative impact.

6. For each action, assign one person (not a team) overall responsibility for the execution of each action.

7. Lastly, identify a date to complete the implementation of each action.

(continued)

Sample Risk Analysis Tool

Key Risks	Probability of Impact (H, M, L)	Severity of Impact (H, M, L)	Consequences	Response	Resp.	Comp. Date
Resources not allocated that were planned or requested (e.g., provide FT communications people, employees from Research & Policy for process documentation)	X	X	Reduced buy-in, considerable confusion, reduced confidence in project team	Review overall work plan and recommend resource reallocations. Review resource requirements for each project team and make recommendations to PMO.	R. Richards	24-Mar
Critical Path Management not being used	X	X	Possible delays at go-live, additional resistance	Project plan being updated with more detail. Will focus additional effort managing work interdependencies between work streams and where critical handoffs are occurring. On a weekly basis, PMO will enhance reporting capability regarding monitoring project progress and personnel assignments. CPM will be implemented immediately.	N. Thanjan	7-Apr

(continued)

Blank Risk Analysis Tool

Key Risks	Probability of Impact (H, M, L)	Severity of Impact (H, M, L)	Consequences	Response	Resp.	Comp. Date

Role-to-Job Mapping Tool

What is it and when should it be used?

This is one of the more sophisticated tools and should only be used when working with someone who is very experienced in organization design. The role-to-job mapping tool is used to assign business roles to positions in the redesigned organization. Conceptually, the tool provides the bridge between organization and job redesign.

Depending on the scope of the organizational design, it may be important to approach role-to-job mapping from a macro perspective. This would include an activity grouping by department, which would show which department is accountable for certain activities.

The role-to-job mapping tool should be used during the Design phase when completing Detailed Design.

Definitions:

- **Activity:** An activity is a description of how employees allocate their time (e.g., answering phones).

- **Role:** A role consists of a group of activities. For example, a facilitator
  - keeps group discussions on target to meet goals;
  - tracks the length of meetings;
  - provides meeting attendees with a written agenda prior to meetings;
  - writes weekly updates and sends to meeting attendees.

- **Job/ Position:** A job/position consists of all the roles and activities within that position.

How to do it:

1. Complete the Activity Rationalization Template. Use the template to analyze one position at a time. In the first column, list all the activities associated with the job in the "As-Is Activity Field" using current job descriptions. After listing the activities, ask, "What are the other activities not listed on this matrix?" Include any additional activities in the matrix.

2. In the second column, rationalize current activities in light of the future state organizational redesign. Activities can be (only one option should be selected for each activity)

   a. **retained as is.** If this option is selected, it is important to identify which position(s) in the organization will now be responsible for the activity.
   b. **redefined.** If this option is selected, provide an explanation of why the activity will be redefined and who will be responsible for the activity.
   c. **eliminated.** If this option is selected, provide an explanation of why the activity was eliminated.

(continued)

3. Next, refer to the Competency Template by Function to identify the key competencies, organized by the skills, knowledge, and attributes required for each function.

4. Transfer the key competencies from the Competency Template by Function to the left column of the Job/Competency Matrix. To prioritize the competencies, assign a number based on how critical that competency is to the job (1 = Critical, 2 = Very Important, 3 = Important). Completing this step will provide information on the key competencies required for each position.

5. The next step is to analyze all the activities that a manager or VP owns and how these activities are distributed across jobs. List all the activities associated with a process in the column on the left in the Activities to Job Matrix. For instance, the process could be data administration, so all activities related to data administration would be listed. When the processes and corresponding activities are listed, place a checkmark in the template if the activity applies to the job. This will allow the VP or manager to examine the full range of responsibilities associated with each job. Remember to list all processes owned by the relevant manager or VP in the column on the left.

6. This template should also be used for ongoing maintenance. It is important to periodically review the activities associated with each job to ensure that employees are still responsible for the activities to which they had been originally assigned. If not, changes should be made in the template. If any changes are made, be sure to provide detailed comments in the column on the right.

Activity Rationalization Template

Position:		
As-Is Activity	**Future Status of Activity**	**Explanation**

(continued)

Sample Completed Activity Rationalization Matrix

Position: Director—Operations		
As-Is Activity	**Future Status of Activity**	**Explanation**
Develop metrics and integrate into a dashboard.	**Redefined.** Will be integrated into other management reports. The Director of Management Reporting in Finance will now be responsible for this.	Consolidating all planning and progress reporting into one function to obtain an economy of scale. Expected savings are three FTEs.
Document and streamline processes.	**Retained as is.** Six Sigma black belt will be responsible for this.	Activity will still be completed as in the past, but will reduce costs by better leveraging technical support so that this position is about 50% strategic and 50% tactical.
Manage internal productivity projects with a capital budget in excess of $5M.	**Eliminated.**	Contract with external vendor and outsource this functionality. Can be obtained in the outside market for an average hourly cost of $300/hour. Expect to save $450K annually.

(continued)

Competency Template by Function

Competencies		
Skills	**Knowledge**	**Attributes**

Sample Completed Competency Template by Function

Competencies		
Skills	**Knowledge**	**Attributes**
Conceptual thinking	Integrated circuit board technology	Attention to detail
Written and verbal communications	Electronics industry	Sense of urgency
Results focus	Six Sigma	
Analytical skills	World class manufacturing	
Relationship management		

(continued)

Job/Competency Matrix

Competencies	Job #1	Job #2	Job #3	Job #4	Job #5	Job #6	Job #7	Job #8	Job #9	Comments

Legend: 1 = Critical, 2 = Very Important, 3 = Important

Sample Completed Job/Competency Matrix

Competencies	Director of Operations	Manager of Operations	Production Manager	Supervisor	Team Leader
Strategic thinking	1	2	3	3	3
Problem solving	2	2	1	1	1
Verbal communications	2	2	1	1	1
Written communications	2	2	3	3	3
Analytical skills	3	2	1	1	1

Legend: 1 = Critical, 2 = Very Important, 3 = Important

(continued)

Activities to Job Matrix

Activity (by process)	Functional Areas									Comments
	Job #1	Job #2	Job #3	Job #4	Job #5	Job #6	Job #7	Job #8	Job #9	

Completed Activities to Job Matrix

Recruiting Activities	HR Partner	Recruiting	Hiring Manager	Director Finance			
Update position specs	X		X				
Confirm headcount				X			
Create sourcing strategy		X					
Place ads in recruiting channels		X					
Screen candidates	X	X					
Complete interviews	X		X				
Check references	X						
Negotiate offer	X		X				
Bring new hire on board	X						

Talent Assessment Retention Tool

What is it and when should it be used?

This tool can be used to identify key talent, forecast the loss of key talent, and develop a talent retention plan. It is most commonly used during the Define phase during Organize Project.

How to do it:

Steps for Overall Talent Assessment

Steps	Tool
1. Develop clear definition of "key talent." Use definition to objectively identify specific individuals who are classified as key talent.	See Section I: Key Talent Identification Worksheet
Obtain final consensus on which jobs are included within "key talent."	
Key talent positions are not just senior management, but individuals who possess critical relationships with suppliers/customers, possess unique/mission critical skills, and/or are part of a function/department that is very strategic to the organization.	
2. Identify the specific competencies that are critical to ensuring continued success of the business.	See Section II: Competency Evaluation Worksheet
Set quantitative retention goals and hold executives accountable.	
3. Steering team force ranks talent	See Section III: Talent Assessment Questions
Review appropriate documentation (succession plans, past performance appraisals, notes in personnel file, track record on completing projects, etc.).	
Have each function identify top performers.	
Rank employees according to competencies needed in the future.	

(continued)

Steps for Overall Talent Assessment *(concluded)*

Steps	Tool
4. Categorize all employees into the following categories:	See Section IV: Retention Planning Template
Strong performer, must retain	
Okay in present job, but needs development	
Should be in job with less scope	
Transition immediately	
5. Complete talent loss forecast.	See Section V: Talent Loss Assessment Worksheet
Identify key talent that is most likely to leave as well as identify talent gaps across the organization.	
6. Identify retention strategies and develop a customized retention plan for each key talent.	See Section VI: Best Practices Retention Strategies See also Section IV: Retention Planning Template
Periodically review talent retention results and conduct cause analysis to determine remedial actions.	

(continued)

Section I: Key Talent Identification Worksheet

Purpose: This worksheet can be used to identify key talent through objective application of the key talent criteria.

Decision Makers

Employees	President	COO	CFO	VP HR	VP Sales				

Key questions to ask to objectively identify key talent:

1. Is he or she a member of senior management?
2. Does he or she possess key relationships with suppliers, customers, etc.?
3. Does he or she possess unique or mission critical skills or is he or she part of a very strategic function/department?
4. Is he or she typically assigned the most critical or difficult projects?

(continued)

Section II: Competency Evaluation Worksheet

Purpose: This worksheet can be used to assess key talent within the organization.

Competencies

Employees	Competency 1	Competency 2	Competency 3	Competency 4	Competency 5					Total

Key:

3 = Incumbent possesses strong capability relative to this competency.

2 = Incumbent possesses moderate capability relative to this competency.

1 = Incumbent possesses low capability relative to this competency.

(continued)

Section III: Talent Assessment Questions

Purpose: This worksheet can be used to assess key talent.

	Assessment Questions
1	What are the employee's strengths/weaknesses?
2	What specifically accounts for the employee's effectiveness?
3	What is the employee's long-term growth potential?
4	What are the employee's major accomplishments?
5	What have been the biggest problems in managing the employee?
6	What is the next logical career step for the employee?
7	What type of environment does the employee work best/worst in?
8	How can the employee be best motivated?
9	Who are the key backers or advocates this employee has in the company?
10	How is the employee likely to respond to the organization redesign? What does he/she stand to gain or lose?
11	What problems, risks, or benefits would this employee cause if he/she left? (Lose key customer relationships, loss of critical intellectual capital, loss of proprietary skills, etc.)?
12	What is the probability that the employee will stay with the company? How will the employee adapt to the new organization?
13	Who, if anyone, could replace this employee if he/she leaves?
14	Categorize the employee as must retain, necessary to keep during the transition, not critical whether leaves or remains, or should be terminated in the short term.

(continued)

Section IV: Retention Planning Template

Purpose: This worksheet can be used to develop a retention plan.

Key Employees	Must retain	Okay, needs development	Should be in job with less scope	Terminate	Retention Actions	Responsible Party	Timing

(continued)

Section V: Talent Loss Assessment Worksheet (Sample)

Purpose: This worksheet can be used to forecast the loss of key talent within the organization.

Employees

(High = 3, Medium = 2, Low = 1)	J. James	H. Smith	B. Parks					
Value of Talent								
Degree to which the employee has key relationships with stakeholders	3	2	3					
Importance of employee to organization performance or redesign success	3	2	1					
Difficulty in finding a replacement	3	2	3					
Uniqueness of competencies	3	2	1					
Confidence position can be covered in a more cost-effective manner	1	2	3					
Risk of Talent Loss								
Confidence that "golden handcuffs" are already in place	1	2	3					
Degree to which employee has a perception the redesign will result in negative role change	1	2	3					
Degree to which employee strongly supports the organization design	1	2	3					
Degree to which existing culture remains stable	1	2	3					
Go forward compensation and career path are perceived as being a "take away" and are not equal to or above industry norms	1	2	3					
Scoring:	18	20	26					

Risk of Loss: (High = 24–30, **Medium** = 15–23, **Low** = <15)

(continued)

Section VI: Best Practices Retention Strategies

Purpose: This worksheet can be used to identify and apply best practices talent retention strategies.

	Listed below are best practices retention strategies that leading companies commonly use. Research studies have concluded that nonfinancial strategies tend to work better than financial strategies.
1.0	**Provide direct supervisor intervention.** This should occur as soon as possible in the organization redesign process. Assurances should be made to critical talent: (1) they have a job in the future, (2) their importance to the company is understood. Clarify future job role and career ladder and provide constant communications with employees regarding their concerns throughout the entire redesign process.
2.0	**Use nonfinancial bonus and incentive programs.** There are a number of incentives such as tickets to the theater, dinner awards, and additional vacation days that can be used that have a nominal cost but convey your concern for these employees.
3.0	**Redesign jobs of critical talent.** This could include (1) title change and (2) increase autonomy, responsibility, and/or authority.
4.0	**Create employment value proposition and brand.** According to the corporate executive board, there are distinct changes in employee job offer/retention preferences since 1999. Employees are voicing the following job attributes as being increasingly important: (1) manager quality, (2) external equity, (3) bonus, (4) amount of travel, (5) promotional opportunity, (6) internal equity, (7) flexible work opportunities. It is important for the organization to communicate to employees the value of what it offers to the employee (employment value proposition relative to each of the above seven items). Stress the advantages of the compensation and benefits program, work-life balance, company culture and credo, financial vitality of the organization, etc.
5.0	**Hold managers accountable for retention.** Regularly examine the involuntary turnover rates to assess trends and underlying root causes. Determine why critical employees left. Assess what was done to retain each employee and modify approach situationally.
6.0	**Complete career development meetings for key talent.** Ask key talent the following questions: (1) What are your short- and mid-term career aspirations? (2) What specific actions can we both undertake to develop a pathway that is a win-win for you and the organization? Additional actions can include: (A) clarifying performance goals, (B) solidifying knowledge and understanding of the organization, (C) providing additional career development opportunities (job rotations, developmental assignments, etc.) as needed.

(continued)

Section VI: Best Practices Retention Strategies *(concluded*

7.0	**Schedule executive outreach.** The appropriate executive will schedule an informal breakfast or lunch with critical employees who have a high flight risk. The focus of the discussions is to clarify the importance of the individual to the organization, identify any concerns the individual may have, and work aggressively toward actions that will mitigate those concerns. Once the meetings have been conducted, it is a good idea to provide ongoing access/visibility to key members of senior management.
8.0	**Offer mentor pairing.** Key employees are matched with an executive mentor to both demonstrate their importance to the organization as well as enhance the probability of success in the new design.
9.0	**Conduct new leader assimilation.** An interactive meeting is conducted with the direct reports of a new leader to discuss what they know/want to know about the new leader, what they need from the leader to be successful, and what their key priorities are.
10.0	**Use financial bonus and incentive programs.** There are a number of financial incentives such as (1) bonuses tied to completion of redesign and realization of targeted results, (2) spot awards, (3) stock option grants, (4) base compensation increases, (5) enhanced benefits, (6) promotion, (7) enhanced severance package.

Team Competency Matrix

What is it and when should it be used?

This tool should be used by team leaders of organization design work stream teams prior to completing the initial team chartering. It is most commonly used during the Define phase during Organize Project and during points in the project when additional teams are created. This tool can be used to

1. identify what competencies are needed for the team to be successful in achieving its charter;
2. select the most appropriate people to participate in the team;
3. identify skill gaps and determine specific activities to address new competency attainment.

How to do it:

Listed below are the steps for developing and using a team competency matrix (a blank template and completed sample are on the following page).

1. **Brainstorm the competencies the team needs.** Prior to completing a team charter, use this tool to identify the specific competencies the *overall* team must possess to be successful. Insert these competencies on the top of columns two through six.

2. **Determine competency levels needed across the team.** In row two, identify the level of the competency that is needed *across* the team. Level can be delineated in a number of ways (low, medium, or high; or novice, intermediate, or expert).

3. **Identify potential team members.** List potential team members in column one under the Team Member header. Most teams have core and ad hoc members. Research studies strongly indicate that there is a positive correlation between team size and team performance. Most teams perform best when membership is less than ten individuals.

4. **Evaluate potential team members relative to the needed competencies.** Using available data (e.g., past performance appraisals, input from supervisors), evaluate each potential team member against the desired competencies. Make final selections based on the required competencies, *not* availability. In the completed sample, one could easily ask why Rafael Palmero is on the team since his competencies don't map closely with the needs of the team. Once this step has been completed, then make final team member selections.

5 **Integrate knowledge transfer into the team work plan.** Identify specific actions to remediate competency gaps. This can include coaching, formal educational workshops, and self-study.

(continued)

Team Competency Matrix

Requirements						
Team Members						

Completed Team Competency Matrix

	Change Management	Process Improvement	Benchmarking	Project Management	Enabling Information Tech.	Facilitation
Requirements	H	M	M	M	L–M	H
Team Members						
Tom Smith	M	H	M	L	L	L
Rafael Palmero	L	L	M	L	L	L
Tino Martinez	L	H	M	L	L	L
Tom McIntosh	L	H	L	M	M	L
Robinson Cano	M	L	H	H	H	H
Mary Smith	L	L	H	H	L	H

L = Low, **M** = Medium, **H** = High

Service Level Agreements (SLAs)

What is it and when should it be used?

A service level agreement is a written document that explicitly states the objectives, roles, responsibilities, timing, and quality of handoffs within or between organizations. Service level agreements have specific components that make them useful tools for managing processes. Some common components of a service level agreement include the following:

- The specific products/services that will be delivered
- Decision rights, roles, and responsibilities
- Performance expectations

Service level agreements are used to document the performance expectations when there is an implicit supplier-customer relationship. One of the ways to ensure that the cross-functional cooperation and handoffs are as smooth as possible is to develop service level agreements and standard operating procedures.

This tool is most commonly used during the Define phase when completing Detailed Design and throughout the Implement phase of work.

How to do it:

There are three basic approaches to developing service level agreements:

- Process maps
- Activity charts
- Rolled-up task analysis

Steps:

1. **Document the underlying process.** A process can be conceptualized as a chain with multiple links. Each link represents activities that are completed by a discrete work unit. Most units within large corporations have historically focused myopically on only the links they "own" as opposed to the entire chain. This creates sub-optimization and a silo orientation.

   When redesigning an organization it is critical to document and, if appropriate, redesign processes to ensure they are aligned with the future state structure. SLAs then cascade from both the new structure and redesigned processes.

2. **Jointly agree on the format of the SLA.** A SLA is in reality a contract that formalizes a business relationship. Care should be exercised to not "over engineer" the contract since this is a very labor intensive activity. Focus on the minimum amount of specification that will facilitate your core products/services that are being delivered efficiently and effectively. See the next page for an example of a simple SLA format.

(continued)

Sample Service Level Agreement Format

Service objectives	Setting the expectations of the customer Setting the expectation of the service provider Providing a means of measuring service quality achievements Encouraging a ***service quality*** culture
Parties involved	Who is involved in this service agreement?
Points of contact	Where are the handoffs located and what people, systems, or organizations are involved?
Activities	What activities are being performed?
Deliverables	What products, goods, or services are provided?
Performance measures	What performance measures are used to evaluate the activities or deliverables?
Data sources	What information sources will be used to make the evaluation?
Work flow	What is the work flow between different parties?
Service levels	What are the performance guarantees made by each party?
Renegotiating terms	What rules apply to when and how this agreement can be amended?
Enforcement	Who has the right to enforce the SLA?

3. **Negotiate SLA components.** If not careful, a working relationship can be poisoned by overzealous negotiations. The focus should be on understanding the capabilities and expectations of each party and over time "moving the dials" in the "right" direction. The focus should be on win-win outcomes for all parties.

(continued)

Sample Completed SLA

SLA Title	The Call Center-Payroll Processing Service Level Agreement
Parties involved	HR Call Center, Payroll Production
Service objectives	To ensure that payroll inquiries that need to be investigated get completed within the SLA times allotted, with the highest possible quality, with the least number of boundary crossings
Handoffs	Payroll inquiry and their solutions
Activities	• The Call Center receives a payroll inquiry. • The Call Center opens a case. • The Call Center forwards inquiries that need further inquiry. • Payroll conducts needed inquiry. • Payroll sends inquiry answers/solutions to employee. • Payroll informs the Call Center of its answers/solutions. • Payroll closes the case.
Performance measures	The Call Center owns the case. The Call Center will send inquiries to Payroll Processing within 30 minutes after determining need for inquiry. Payroll will provide an answer to the inquiry within 24 hours. Payroll will send answers/solution to the inquiry to the employee within 30 minutes of its discovery. Payroll will close the case and send confirmation to the Call Center case owner.
Data sources	All case management documentation to be found in Expert Advisor.
Renegotiating terms	Both Call Center and Payroll Processing management must be in agreement to which terms should be renegotiated. Points *requiring* renegotiation include the following: • Failure to meet performance measures seven days in a row • 25 percent increase in the number of inquiries over a quarter • HR service management's call for renegotiation • LOB call for renegotiation
Enforcement	The head of the Service Center

(continued)

Blank Service Level Agreement Template

Service objectives	
Parties involved	
Points of contact	
Activities	
Deliverables	
Performance measures	
Data sources	
Work flow	
Service levels	
Renegotiating terms	
Enforcement	

Staffing Estimation Template

What is it and when should it be used?

This tool is most commonly used during the Design phase during Detailed Design. It can be used to estimate the number of full-time and part-time equivalents who are needed at either the **role** or **job** level of analysis.

How to do it:

1. Map roles into discrete jobs.

2. Decompose jobs into activities and tasks.

3. Using historical data, identify the number of times a job completes each activity and task. Identify **average** and **peak** volumes to ensure that you take into account seasonal or cyclical impacts on each job. If historical data is not available, estimate the volumes.

4. Again, referring to past history, identify the average amount of time (in hours) it takes to complete each activity and task. If historical data isn't available, you should collect data from a number of people who complete the task/step on a regular basis. This time data should be normalized based on experience levels, education, etc. The spreadsheet is based on an algorithm that multiplies the average time in hours (or fractions thereof) to complete each task/step by its volume and dividing it by a predetermined number of usable hours per day (assumes 1950 hours of available time per year).

5. Make an assumption regarding the utilization level at which you will target staffing. Refer to historical performance data relative to planned/unplanned absences (sickness, tardiness, vacation) and training.

6. Select one of the following tactics to address peak fluctuations:

   Load leveling. Move work from peak periods to non-peak periods. This can be accomplished via pricing incentives, creating backlogs, or rough work scheduling.

   Cross training. This involves training employees who work in another area to augment capacity. This is appropriate for short duration peaks.

   Overtime. Ask employees to work longer hours. Overtime works best when the peaks are for a short duration.

   Expandable staff. Employ more total people year round, but utilize a portion of these people on a regular, part-time basis. As volumes increase, these people become a flexible resource and can supplement capacity. Since they are part-time, you save on benefits.

   Temporary staff. Add staff only during peak times; when the peak is alleviated, reduce the staff. Potential sources include temp agencies, former employees, or retired employees.

   Staff sharing. Different units that experience peaks at different times lend their staff as needed. Works best for units that are highly integrated.

   Outsourcing. Contract out with an outside agency to perform all or part of the activities.

(continued)

Completed Example

Job	Tasks	Volume		Average Time	Total Time		FTEs	
		Average	Peak	to Complete	Average	Peak	Avg.	Peak
							0.00	0.00
HR Generalist 1	Recruiting	50	70	10.00	500	700	0.26	0.36
	Performance mgt	77	110	1.00	77	110	0.04	0.06
	Organization design	25	40	30.00	750	1200	0.38	0.62
	Employee relations	79	150	0.50	39.5	75	0.02	0.04
					0	0	0.00	0.00
					0	0	0.00	0.00
					0	0	0.00	0.00
					0	0	0.00	0.00
					0	0	0.00	0.00
					0	0	0.00	0.00
					0	0	0.00	0.00
					0	0	0.00	0.00
					0	0	0.00	0.00
					0	0	0.00	0.00
					0	0	0.00	0.00
					0	0	0.00	0.00
					0	0	0.00	0.00
					0	0	0.00	0.00
					0	0	0.00	0.00
					0	0	0.00	0.00
					0	0	0.00	0.00
Totals		231.0	370.0	41.5	1366.5	2085.0	0.70	1.08

(continued)

Blank Template

Job	Tasks	Volume		Average Time	Total Time		FTEs	
		Average	Peak	to Complete	Average	Peak	Avg.	Peak
							0.00	0.00
					0	0	0.00	0.00
					0	0	0.00	0.00
					0	0	0.00	0.00
					0	0	0.00	0.00
					0	0	0.00	0.00
					0	0	0.00	0.00
					0	0	0.00	0.00
					0	0	0.00	0.00
					0	0	0.00	0.00
					0	0	0.00	0.00
					0	0	0.00	0.00
					0	0	0.00	0.00
					0	0	0.00	0.00
					0	0	0.00	0.00
					0	0	0.00	0.00
					0	0	0.00	0.00
					0	0	0.00	0.00
					0	0	0.00	0.00
					0	0	0.00	0.00
					0	0	0.00	0.00
Totals		0.0	0.0	0.0	0.0	0.0	0.0	0.0

Standard Operating Procedure (SOP)

What is it and when should it be used?

A standard operating procedure is a written document that details *how* a discrete piece of work is to be completed.

SOPs and service level agreements are commonly used in conjunction with one another to guide staff in how to execute work during the implementation process.

This tool is most commonly used during the Define phase when completing Detailed Design and throughout the Implement phase of work.

How to do it:

Steps:

1. **Review available documentation.** Review any relevant documentation that describes how work is completed in the current state. This can include such things as administrative policies, job descriptions, process documentation, management reports, and performance metrics. Assess their applicability to the future state.

2. **Jointly agree on the format of the SOP.** Document the SOP from the perspective of what a new hire with limited job understanding would need to know to successfully perform on the job. See the samples on the following pages for an example of a simple SOP format and a sample completed SOP.

3. **Update the SOP appropriately.** Using relevant data inputs (future state structure charts, updated position descriptions, updated process documentation, RCI charts, etc.), fill in the SOP templates. Vet the drafts with current job incumbents and test the SOPs to ensure that they are accurate and actionable.

(continued)

Sample SOP Format

Description	The description section names the procedure, identifies what initiates the procedure, and provides a general description of the roles and responsibilities of each individual involved in the procedure.
Procedure detail	The section provides a detailed narrative and/or graphic description of the procedure. The detail must be sufficient enough so that most individuals would know how to accomplish the procedure with minimal help.
Security issues	This section describes any security issues that are manifested in the procedures, such as password, access privileges, access timing, etc.
Audit requirements	In some procedures, it is necessary to separate duties within the procedure. For example, when a nonactive employee remits a check to HRS Finance for benefits payment, the check is posted by one individual and confirmed by another.
Compliance issues	In some procedures it is necessary to meet legally mandated, recommended, or suggested requirements within the procedure. For example, some individuals may have access to medical information and others may not, depending on compliance requirements of the procedures.
Additional information	This section provides any additional information a Service Center associate may want or need to complete the procedure. This should include specialists, telephone numbers, Intranet or Internet sites, etc.

(continued)

Sample Completed SOP

Handling Difficult Calls

Description

On occasion, a Service Center associate has a situation where communication with the caller is challenging. There are standard approaches defined for several of these situations.

Procedure Detail

If a caller is using abusive language or behavior and it is not possible to carry on a productive conversation, the call may go through an escalation process:

1. The Service Center associate transfers the call to a project manager or unit manager.
2. If the behavior continues, the manager informs the caller that the call will be ended and states the reason.
3. If the behavior continues, the manager disconnects the call and logs the information in TBA Notes and Call Tracker.
4. Alternatively, the Service Center associates may perform the last two steps if they feel comfortable with it.

Additional Information

Irate Callers

If a caller is angry and requests to speak with a manager, or if the Service Center associate feels it is necessary, the call may go through an escalation process.

Escalation Process

1. The Service Center associate transfers the call to a project manager.
2. The manager transfers the call to a unit manager.
3. The unit manager transfers the call to a PSM or Tom Flint.

Callers at Risk

"Callers at risk" refers to callers who are threatening or alluding to harm themselves or others.

(continued)

Sample Completed SOP *(concluded)*

While on the Call

1. Take all threats as serious ones.
2. Do not ignore the threat! Talk to the caller about what they have said; it will be a way to find out how serious they are.
3. Show empathy! Let them know that you care about their welfare.
4. Talk to the participant long enough that you both feel comfortable hanging up.

Organization	Service	Telephone Number
Call for Help *	24-hour service line	(618) XXX-XXXX
Samaritans	Crisis intervention	(617) XXX-XXXX
Youth Suicide	National center	(415) XXX-XXXX

About the Author

Ronald Recardo ronald.recardo@gmail.com has over 25 years of global corporate executive and management consulting experience. During that time. he has worked with over 100 different companies, including Johnson & Johnson, Fidelity Investments, General Electric, Schick-Wilkinson Sword, VNU, and Pennsylvania Power & Light. In his role as advisor to senior executives, he provides counsel on strategic consulting, change management, and human resources issues.

Ronald is the author of over 30 articles and books. In addition to his writing, he has had considerable public speaking experience before such groups as the American Management Association, the Association for Quality and Participation, the Association for Manufacturing Excellence, The Conference Board, American Production and Inventory Control Society, and the OD Network. He is a member of American Mensa, Ltd., and is listed in the International WHO'S WHO of Professionals and the WHO'S WHO of Entrepreneurs. He is one of only 3,000 certified management consultants (CMC) in the world, which is the highest accreditation awarded in the management consulting profession.

www.ingramcontent.com/pod-product-compliance
Lightning Source LLC
Chambersburg PA
CBHW080558220326
41599CB00032B/6532